"*Founders and Prophets* brings together in one book all of my favorite quotes from my favorite and most trusted sources. As a parent, I love how it is organized because it helps me teach these principles to my children in simple, yet powerful and engaging ways they enjoy. I highly recommend this book to any who want to be inspired about the godly gift of liberty!"

Senator Alvin Jackson

Founders & Prophets

12 Principles of Freedom

Brought to life through clauses, quotes, scriptures, and short stories

By Jeff Hymas

with contributions by ShaRee Hymas
and short stories compiled by Marlene Peterson

Distributed by Ringmasters Media
2437 N Rulon White Blvd.
Ogden UT 84404

Cover design by Jeff Wolfley and Shannon Dejong

Edited by: Heather Godfrey
Layout by: Kirk Edwards

ISBN: 978-1-942298-14-4

Dedicated to the wives and to the children of
our founding fathers and prophets
whose depth of personal sacrifice, though not
as public, was just as monumental

Table of Contents

INTRODUCTION

People often say to me, "I hate politics!" To them I say, "I do too!" This book is not political and it does not support either traditional party, but it does support the principles of freedom and it does support the family, which is the most effective organization for teaching and preserving those principles.

After four years of traveling thousands of miles teaching hundreds of presentations on the Constitution, I am convinced that the most important group that needs to hear the message of freedom is the youth and that the most effective way to get it into their hearts and minds is through their families. I'm also convinced that parents don't feel like they have the tools they need to teach freedom in a way that makes it relevant and appealing in their children's lives (or in their own lives for that matter). This book is written to give Latter-day Saint parents the tools they need to first understand freedom themselves and then to be able to teach it to their children.

We need to bridge the gap between what we feel about freedom and what we know about it because we can't truly love what we don't understand. I believe that the surest way to gain an understanding of freedom and its importance in our lives is to define and explore principles—the simple, fundamental declarations of truth that serve as the foundation for our belief systems. Principles are timeless. Principles don't change with public opinion polls nor do they grow irrelevant any more than gravity yields itself to the results of popularity contests or to the passage of time. Viewing our world through the lens of those principles—no matter how tempting it is to see modern-day issues as special circumstances that require exceptions to the rule—provides us with a clear vision and a sure foundation upon which to build our understanding of government's proper role in our lives. The twelve principles of freedom I chose as the structure for this book represent the most basic of truths upon which our system of government was organized. Exploring their definitions through the words of founders and prophets and seeing the interconnectivity and consistency between them is to see the Lord's hand in the establishment of these principles of freedom in our country's founding documents.

My original intent with this book was to make it as thorough and comprehensive as possible, so I gathered every quote and reference I could get my hands on. However, my wise wife convinced me that its power would be in its simplicity. With that end in mind, I designed each chapter to just have one scriptural reference, one constitutional reference, one prophetic quote and one founding father quote along with a short story to support each principle and bring it to life. Then, with some help from some brilliant contributors, I added a section to help adapt the principle to families, and placed all the other quotes and references in an appendix, organized by principle, for additional study and insight. The end result is an easy-to-use format that I hope will benefit you as you learn and share the principles of freedom.

My desire is that Latter-day Saint families will spend time together taking a fresh look at freedom and that they will gain a stronger and more personal testimony of the principles that provided for the founding of our nation and for the restoration of the gospel. I hope that you will be inspired, as I have been, at the complementary and cohesive witnesses amongst founders and prophets which stand as unwavering pillars in the politically turbulent world we live in.

The overarching purpose of this book is to instill in each reader a love and a respect for our prophets and our founding fathers and their respective works in scripture and in our founding documents, a greater reverence and appreciation for the principles of freedom, and a deeper sense of worship for and gratitude towards the authors of all freedom—our Father in Heaven and His Son, Jesus Christ. If this book accomplishes such an end it will have fulfilled its purpose.

"May those principles, which were so honorably and nobly defended, namely, the Constitution of our land, by our fathers, be established forever."

-Joseph Smith

Dedicatory prayer of the first latter-day temple
March 27, 1836, Kirtland, Ohio

Principle 1
PROPER ROLE OF GOVERNMENT

Freedom is best preserved when men form government to operate within its proper role of protecting rights.

EXPLANATION:

We believe that governments are instituted of God for the benefit of man (D&C 134:1), therefore we believe that government is absolutely necessary to provide a civil and free society. Since government is the power delegated by man to act with force on others, governmental power should only be used in circumstances in which an individual would use force, such as protecting his life, his liberty and his property. Government in its proper realm should be protective rather than proactive. It should be negative (punishing and acting against those who have infringed on others' rights) rather than positive (taking from some to give to others). If government were to operate only within its proper role, then it would *not* be in a position to be used as an instrument of advantage and gain. Government would exist to simply provide equal protection under the law to all its citizens, so that each could go about his life promoting his own best interest in ways that would not infringe on the rights of others.

FROM THE CONSTITUTION:

"That to secure these rights Governments are instituted among men."

Declaration of Independence

FROM THE FOUNDING FATHERS:

"The policy of the American government is to leave their citizens free, neither restraining nor aiding them in their pursuits."

Thomas Jefferson[1]

---

1 John P. Foley, ed., *The Jeffersonian Cyclopedia: A Comprehensive Collection of the Views of Thomas Jefferson* (London: Funk & Wagnalls Company, 1900), 500.

FROM THE PROPHETS:

"There is one simple test. Do I as an individual have a right to use force upon my neighbor to accomplish this goal? If I do have such a right, then I may delegate that power to my government to exercise on my behalf. If I do not have that right as an individual, then I cannot delegate it to government, and I cannot ask my government to perform the act for me. To be sure, there are times when this principle of the proper role of government is most annoying and inconvenient. If I could only FORCE the ignorant to provide for themselves, or the selfish to be generous with their wealth! But if we permit government to manufacture its own authority out of thin air, and to create self-proclaimed powers not delegated to it by the people, then the creature exceeds the creator and becomes master."

Ezra Taft Benson[2]

FROM THE SCRIPTURES:

"And that law of the land which is constitutional, *supporting that principle of freedom in maintaining rights and privileges*, belongs to all mankind, and is justifiable before me. Therefore, I, the Lord, justify you, and your brethren of my church, in befriending that law which is the constitutional law of the land; And as pertaining to law of man, whatsoever is more or less than this, cometh of evil."

Doctrine and Covenants 98:5-7, (*emphasis added)*

STORY TO ILLUSTRATE THE PRINCIPLE:

Davy Crockett – Not Yours to Give

James J. Bethune [pseud.], *Not Yours to Give* (Harper's Magazine, 1867).
Original grammar and spelling maintained.

One day in the House of Representatives, a bill was taken up appropriating money for the benefit of a widow of a distinguished naval officer. Several beautiful speeches had been made in its support. The Speaker was just about to put the question when Davy Crockett arose:

"Mr. Speaker–I have as much respect for the memory of the deceased, and as much sympathy for the sufferings of the living, if

2 Ezra T. Benson, *The Proper Role of Government* (1968).

suffering there be, as any man in this House, but we must not permit our respect for the dead or our sympathy for a part of the living to lead us into an act of injustice to the balance of the living. I will not go into an argument to prove that Congress has no power to appropriate this money as an act of charity. Every member upon this floor knows it. We have the right, as individuals, to give away as much of our own money as we please in charity; but as members of Congress we have no right so to appropriate a dollar of the public money. Some eloquent appeals have been made to us upon the ground that it is a debt due the deceased. Mr. Speaker, the deceased lived long after the close of the war; he was in office to the day of his death, and I have never heard that the government was in arrears to him.

Every man in this House knows it is not a debt. We cannot, without the grossest corruption, appropriate this money as the payment of a debt. We have not the semblance of authority to appropriate it as a charity. Mr. Speaker, I have said we have the right to give as much money of our own as we please. I am the poorest man on this floor. I cannot vote for this bill, but I will give one week's pay to the object, and if every member of Congress will do the same, it will amount to more than the bill asks."

He took his seat. Nobody replied. The bill was put upon its passage, and, instead of passing unanimously, as was generally supposed, and as, no doubt, it would, but for that speech, it received but few votes, and, of course, was lost.

Later, when asked by a friend why he had opposed the appropriation, Crockett gave this explanation:

"Several years ago I was one evening standing on the steps of the Capitol with some other members of Congress, when our attention was attracted by a great light over in Georgetown. It was evidently a large fire. We jumped into a hack and drove over as fast as we could. In spite of all that could be done, many houses were burned and many families made homeless, and, besides, some of them had lost all but the clothes they had on. The weather was very cold, and when I saw so many women and children suffering, I felt that something ought to be done for them. The next morning a bill was introduced appropriating $20,000 for their relief. We put aside all other business and rushed it through as soon as it could be done.

"The next summer, when it began to be time to think about the election, I concluded I would take a scout around among the boys of my district. I had no opposition there, but, as the election was some time off, I did not know what might turn up. When riding one day in a part of my district in which I was more of a stranger than any other, I saw a man in a field plowing and coming toward the road. I gauged my gait so that we should meet as he came to the fence. As he came up, I spoke to the man. He replied politely, but, as I thought, rather coldly.

"I began: 'Well, friend, I am one of those unfortunate beings called candidates, and–'

"'Yes, I know you; you are Colonel Crockett, I have seen you once before, and voted for you the last time you were elected. I suppose you are out electioneering now, but you had better not waste your time or mine. I shall not vote for you again.'

"This was a sockdolager . . . I begged him to tell me what was the matter.

"'Well, Colonel, it is hardly worth-while to waste time or words upon it. I do not see how it can be mended, but you gave a vote last winter which shows that either you have not capacity to understand the Constitution, or that you are wanting in the honesty and firmness to be guided by it. In either case you are not the man to represent me. But I beg your pardon for expressing it in that way. I did not intend to avail myself of the privilege of the constituent to speak plainly to a candidate for the purpose of insulting or wounding you. I intend by it only to say that your understanding of the Constitution is very different from mine; and I will say to you what, but for my rudeness, I should not have said, that I believe you to be honest. . . . But an understanding of the Constitution different from mine I cannot overlook, because the Constitution, to be worth anything, must be held sacred, and rigidly observed in all its provisions. The man who wields power and misinterprets it is the more dangerous the more honest he is.'

"'I admit the truth of all you say, but there must be some mistake about it, for I do not remember that I gave any vote last winter upon any constitutional question.'

"'No, Colonel, there's no mistake. Though I live here in the backwoods and seldom go from home, I take the papers from Washington and read very carefully all the proceedings of Congress. My papers say that last winter you voted for a bill to appropriate $20,000 to some sufferers by a fire in Georgetown. Is that true?'

"'Well, my friend; I may as well own up. You have got me there. But certainly nobody will complain that a great and rich country like ours should give the insignificant sum of $20,000 to relieve its suffering women and children, particularly with a full and overflowing Treasury, and I am sure, if you had been there, you would have done just as I did.'

"'It is not the amount, Colonel, that I complain of; it is the principle. In the first place, the government ought to have in the Treasury no more than enough for its legitimate purposes. But that has nothing to do with the question. The power of collecting and disbursing money at pleasure is the most dangerous power that can be intrusted to man, particularly under our system of collecting revenue by a tariff, which reaches every man in the country, no matter how poor he may be, and the poorer he is the more he pays in proportion to his means. What is worse, it presses upon him without his knowledge where the weight centers, for there is not a man in the United States who can ever guess how much he pays to the government. So you see, that while you are contributing to relieve one, you are drawing it from thousands who are even worse off than he. If you had the right to give anything, the amount was simply a matter of discretion with you, and you had as much right to give $20,000,000 as $20,000. If you have the right to give to one, you have the right to give to all; and, as the Constitution neither defines charity nor stipulates the amount, you are at liberty to give to any and everything which you may believe, or profess to believe, is a charity, and to any amount you may think proper. You will very easily perceive what a wide door this would open for fraud and corruption and favoritism, on the one hand, and for robbing the people on the other. No, Colonel, Congress has no right to give charity. Individual members may give as much of their own money as they please, but they have no right to touch a dollar of the public money for that purpose. If twice as many houses had been burned in this county as in Georgetown, neither you nor any other member of Congress would have thought of appropriating a dollar for our relief. There are about two hundred and forty members of Congress. If they had shown their sympathy for the sufferers by contributing each one week's pay, it would have made over $13,000. There are plenty of wealthy men in and around Washington who could have given $20,000 without depriving themselves of even a luxury of life. The congressmen chose to keep their own money, which, if reports be true, some of them spend not very creditably; and the people about Washington, no doubt, applauded you for relieving them from the necessity of giving by giving what was not yours to give. The people have delegated to Congress, by the Constitution, the power to do certain things. To do these, it is authorized to collect and pay moneys, and for nothing else. Everything beyond this is usurpation, and a violation of the Constitution.

"'So you see, Colonel, you have violated the Constitution in what I consider a vital point. It is a precedent fraught with danger to the country, for when Congress once begins to stretch its power beyond the limits of the Constitution, there is no limit to it, and no security for the people. I have no doubt you acted honestly, but that does not make it any better, except as far as you are personally concerned, and you see that I cannot vote for you.'

"I tell you I felt streaked. I saw if I should have opposition, and this man should go to talking, he would set others to talking, and in that district I was a gone fawn-skin. I could not answer him, and the fact is, I was so fully convinced that he was right, I did not want to. But I must satisfy him, and I said to him:

"'Well, my friend, you hit the nail upon the head when you said I had not sense enough to understand the Constitution. I intended to be guided by it, and thought I had studied it fully. I have heard many speeches in Congress about the powers of Congress, but what you have said here at your plow has got more hard, sound sense in it than all the fine speeches I ever heard. If I had ever taken the view of it that you have, I would have put my head into the fire before I would have given that vote; and if you will forgive me and vote for me again, if I ever vote for another unconstitutional law I wish I may be shot.'

"He laughingly replied: 'Yes, Colonel, you have sworn to that once before, but I will trust you again upon one condition. You say that you are convinced that your vote was wrong. Your acknowledgment of it will do more good than beating you for it. If, as you go around the district, you will tell people about this vote, and that you are satisfied it was wrong, I will not only vote for you, but will do what I can to keep down opposition, and, perhaps, I may exert some little influence in that way.'

"'If I don't,' said I, 'I wish I may be shot; and to convince you that I am in earnest in what I say I will come back this way in a week or ten days, and if you will get up a gathering of the people, I will make a speech to them. Get up a barbecue, and I will pay for it.'

"'No, Colonel, we are not rich people in this section, but we have plenty of provisions to contribute for a barbecue, and some to spare for those who have none. The push of crops will be over in a few days, and we can then afford a day for a barbecue. This is Thursday; I will see to getting it up on Saturday week. Come to my house on Friday, and we will go together, and I promise you a very respectable crowd to see and hear you.'

"'Well, I will be here. But one thing more before I say good-by. I must know your name.'

"'My name is Bunce.'

"'Not Horatio Bunce?'

"'Yes.'

"'Well, Mr. Bunce, I never saw you before, though you say you have seen me, but I know you very well. I am glad I have met you, and very proud that I may hope to have you for my friend.'

"It was one of the luckiest hits of my life that I met him. He mingled but little with the public, but was widely known for his remarkable intelligence and incorruptible integrity, and for a heart brimful and running over with kindness and benevolence, which showed themselves not only in words but in acts. He was the oracle of the whole country around him, and his fame had extended far beyond the circle of his immediate acquaintance. Though I had never met him before, I had heard much of him, and but for this meeting it is very likely I should have had opposition, and had been beaten. One thing is very certain, no man could now stand up in that district under such a vote.

"At the appointed time I was at his house, having told our conversation to every crowd I had met, and to every man I stayed all night with, and I found that it gave the people an interest and a confidence in me stronger than I had ever seen manifested before.

"Though I was considerably fatigued when I reached his house, and, under ordinary circumstances, should have gone early to bed, I kept him up until midnight, talking about the principles and affairs of government, and got more real, true knowledge of them than I had got all my life before.

"I have known and seen much of him since, for I respect him–no, that is not the word–I reverence and love him more than any living man, and I go to see him two or three times every year; and I will tell you, sir, if everyone who professes to be a Christian lived and acted and enjoyed it as he does, the religion of Christ would take the world by storm.

"But to return to my story. The next morning we went to the barbecue, and, to my surprise, found about a thousand men there. I met a good many whom I had not known before, and they and my friend introduced me around until I had got pretty well acquainted–at least, they all knew me.

"In due time notice was given that I would speak to them. They gathered up around a stand that had been erected. I opened my speech by saying:

"'Fellow-citizens–I present myself before you today feeling like a new man. My eyes have lately been opened to truths which ignorance or prejudice, or both, had heretofore hidden from my view. I feel that I can today offer you the ability to render you more valuable service than I have ever been able to render before. I am here today more for the purpose of acknowledging my error than to seek your votes. That I should make this acknowledgment is due to myself as well as to you. Whether you will vote for me is a matter for your consideration only.'

"I went on to tell them about the fire and my vote for the appropriation and then told them why I was satisfied it was wrong. I closed by saying:

"'And now, fellow-citizens, it remains only for me to tell you that the most of the speech you have listened to with so much interest was simply a repetition of the arguments by which your neighbor, Mr.

Bunce, convinced me of my error.

"'It is the best speech I ever made in my life, but he is entitled to the credit for it. And now I hope he is satisfied with his convert and that he will get up here and tell you so.'

"He came upon the stand and said:

"'Fellow-citizens–It affords me great pleasure to comply with the request of Colonel Crockett. I have always considered him a thoroughly honest man, and I am satisfied that he will faithfully perform all that he has promised you today.'

"He went down, and there went up from that crowd such a shout for Davy Crockett as his name never called forth before.

"I am not much given to tears, but I was taken with a choking then and felt some big drops rolling down my cheeks. And I tell you now that the remembrance of those few words spoken by such a man, and the honest, hearty shout they produced, is worth more to me than all the honors I have received and all the reputation I have ever made, or ever shall make, as a member of Congress.

"Now, sir," concluded Crockett, "you know why I made that speech yesterday.

"There is one thing now to which I will call your attention. You remember that I proposed to give a week's pay. There are in that House many very wealthy men–men who think nothing of spending a week's pay, or a dozen of them, for a dinner or a wine party when they have something to accomplish by it. Some of those same men made beautiful speeches upon the great debt of gratitude which the country owed the deceased–a debt which could not be paid by money–and the insignificance and worthlessness of money, particularly so insignificant a sum as $10,000, when weighted against the honor of the nation. Yet not one of them responded to my proposition. Money with them is nothing but trash when it is to come out of the people. But it is the one great thing for which most of them are striving, and many of them sacrifice honor, integrity, and justice to obtain it."

Adapting for Families:

Principle: We have more freedom when government's main job is to protect us.

Simple Explanation: Every person can defend his life and his liberty against anyone trying to take it from him, but no one can control other people or make them do things they don't want to do. It is the same with government. Government can and should defend people, but it shouldn't control people or take things from them because that would make them less free.

Discussion Questions:

1. What specific things did you learn about the proper role of government by reading the Davy Crockett story?
2. In what ways do we see government acting outside its proper role today?

See page 145 in the appendix for more references and quotes about the Proper Role of Government.

Principle 2
CHECKS AND BALANCES

Freedom is best preserved when men form a government which has its powers separated into different entities and its actions are subject to review by those separate entities.

EXPLANATION:

Because we understand the weakness and frailties of all men, even (and maybe better said, *especially*) those who are entrusted to occupy positions of power in public service, we know that such men cannot and should not be trusted with all the functions of government. The power to make laws, to execute those laws, and then to judge cases against the prescribed laws are three separate functions of government that should be performed by three separate governmental entities to ensure that no power becomes too great. Also, each separate entity should be subject to oversight from the other two entities with ultimate authority being exercised by the people themselves.

FROM THE CONSTITUTION:

"All legislative powers herein granted shall be vested in a Congress of the United States"

Article I, Section 1, Clause 1

"The executive power shall be vested in a President of the United States of America"

Article II, Section 1, Clause 1

"The judicial power of the Unites States, shall be vested in one supreme court, and in such inferior courts as the Congress may from time to time ordain and establish"

Article III, Section 1, Clause 1

FROM THE FOUNDING FATHERS:

"But the great security against a gradual concentration of the several powers in the same department, consists in giving to those who administer each department the necessary constitutional means and personal motives to resist encroachments of the others. The provision for defense must in this, as in all other cases, be made commensurate to the danger of attack. Ambition must be made to counteract ambition. The interest of the man must be connected with the constitutional rights of the place. It may be a reflection on human nature, that such devices should be necessary to control the abuses of government. But what is government itself, but the greatest of all reflections on human nature? If men were angels, no government would be necessary. If angels were to govern men, neither external nor internal controls on government would be necessary."

James Madison[1]

FROM THE PROPHETS:

"The Constitution is the greatest document, so far as we know, ever adopted by organized society for their government, outside of the kingdom of God. It furnishes the nation a system of checks and balances for their protection so that any one department of the government, cannot, without losing its sacred foundations, be overcome or subordinated by another."

Joseph Fielding Smith[2]

FROM THE SCRIPTURES:

"And now if ye have judges, and they do not judge you according to the law which has been given, ye can cause that they may be judged of a higher judge. If your higher judges do not judge righteous judgments, ye shall cause that a small number of your lower judges should be gathered together, and they shall judge your higher judges, according to the voice of the people."

Mosiah 29:28-29

---

1 Publius [pseud.], *The Federalist Papers* (1787) Federalist Paper No. 51.

2 Joseph Fielding Smith, *The Progress of Man* (Literary Licensing, LLC, 2013).

STORY TO ILLUSTRATE THE PRINCIPLE:

George Washington Would Not Be King

From: Elbridge S. Brooks, *Historic Americans* (New York: Thomas Y. Crowell & Co., 1899), 46-59, abridged.
Original grammar and spelling maintained.

On a breezy hill-slope, overlooking a broad and beautiful river, there stood a comfortable stone farmhouse–famous throughout America as Washington's headquarters.

Within this stone farmhouse on a pleasant May day in the year 1782, in a long, low room with but one window, sat a noble-looking man. Big-framed, large-featured, strong of face and stout of limb, his general's uniform of buff and blue well displayed his commanding figure, while the natural dignity of his bearing made all about him small by comparison, and noticeable only by contrast. That man was General George Washington, commander-in-chief of the armies of the United States.

The general sat at a long, rough table upon which had just been served a simple meal in keeping with the plainness of the room. The general drummed silently upon the table with his fork or abstractedly picked away at the nut meats, talking meanwhile with his much-loved comrade-in-arms, General Knox, who was dining with him that day.

The general was troubled. For, now that Yorktown had been won and the Republic had triumphed, the strain of the actual strife was over and the soldiers of the new Union had time to grumble and leisure to complain. It is always thus with every victorious army in the space between the close of fighting and the establishment of peace.

In this case there were ample reasons for dissatisfaction and complaint. The freemen of the United States were jealous of a trained army, fearful of its power, and with the lessons of the past in mind, anxious to have it disbanded before it might misuse its strength. Their representatives in Congress shared this anxiety, and yet had no immediate means to pay the arrears due to the soldiers for years of faithful service, or even to satisfy their immediate needs.

Unpaid, poorly fed, and still more poorly clothed, with their families at home suffering for the very necessities of life and longing for the return of the bread-winners, both soldiers and officers chafed under the delays and negligence of an apparently unconcerned Congress and clamored for relief. At times this clamor broke out into indignant demands, even into open revolt, stilled or compromise only by the great influence of Washington, who recognized the injustice of the treatment accorded his veterans, while at the same time he appreciated the financial and political weakness of Congress and the country.

He, too, was aware of the possibility of his trained soldiers for evil, if once they asserted their power and determined, as an army, to take matters into their own hands. Already mutterings of revolt and threats of extreme measures had reached him, and he knew that, should he but speak the word, those mutterings and threats would crystalize into instant action, and the liberty the army had fought for might be turned into anarchy or military despotism. When a man knows his power and is still a patriot, that is a sign of moral as well as of personal greatness.

So, as he talked over the situation with General Knox and sought for some method of relief or of compromise, his great heart was troubled, and he drummed the table abstractedly. Just then Billy, the faithful body-servant, approached him.

"Letters, general," he said. "Colonel Tilghman, sir, says a courier from below has just brought you this," and he handed the general a letter, with the inquiry, "Shall I take it to your study general?"

"No, Billy; if the ladies will pardon me I will read it here," the courteous commander replied; and, on the sign of assent, he turned from the table and began to read the letter.

As he read, a flush sprang to that pale face, and the signs of worry that sometimes marked those strong, calm features gave place to astonishment, anger, and disgust. He read the letter through, laid it down, reread it, and then with a quick motion handed it to General Knox.

"Read that, general," he said, and watching his friend's face resumed again the fork-drumming that was the accompaniment to deep thinking.

"Another, eh?" said Knox, as the first words of the letter met his eye. He looked at the signature. "From Colonel Nicola, at the camp. I've heard him talk before. Well, what does he say?" And the hero of Trenton, Monmouth, and Yorktown, the great general's faithful comrade and friend, dashed through the letter with characteristic speed.

Even as he read, the frown on the face of Washington deepened and then disappeared; the flush of anger reddened perceptibly, and then faded from cheek and brow; dignity and calm came again to a countenance not often marked by the passionate nature that, nevertheless, lay deep in the heart of this remarkable leader of men. Then, as the eyes of Knox sought those of his chief in faith and inquiry, Washington took the letter from his hand and, without a word, rising from the table he passed into the room that served him as a study. The ladies turned an inquiring eye upon the general of artillery.

"His excellency laid no ban upon me, ladies," Knox said in reply to those questioning glances. "I think I betray no confidences when I say that he has received the most singular and uncalled-for letter I have ever known to be sent him. Colonel Nicola, ladies, despairs of the Republic. He urges the general to use the army for the setting-up of an energetic government, and, it would seem, in its name, invites George Washington, of all men, to make himself king of America."

That, indeed, was in substance the contents of the letter brought by special courier to Washington, as he sat at dinner in Newburgh on that May day in 1782. It was the opportunity that had come to great leaders before his day, that has come to them since. Caesar, Cromwell, Napoleon, all were tempted with this dream of power, and each one of them either dallied with it, and compromised, or yielded to it, and fell.

But George Washington was made of nobler stuff than any of these men, great and noble though they were. The dream of sovereign power found no place in his unselfish heart. He hesitated not a moment. Indeed, he spurned the proposition, so Professor Channing assures us, "in a manner which has separated him from all other successful leaders in civil strife since the days of the Roman republic." At once he despatched his answer to the veteran who had sought to swerve him from the duty of patriotism.

"With a mixture of surprise and astonishment," he wrote Colonel Nicola, "I have read with attention the sentiments you have submitted to my perusal. Be assured, sire, no occurrence in the course of the war has given me more painful sensations than your information of there being such ideas existing in the army as you have expressed, and which I must view with abhorrence and reprehend with severity...I am much at a loss to conceive what part of my conduct could have given encouragement to such an address, which to me seems big with the greatest mischiefs that can befall my country. If I am not deceived in the knowledge of myself you could not have found a person to whom your schemes are more disagreeable....Let me conjure you, if you have any regard for your country, concern for yourself or posterity, or respect for me, banish these thoughts from your mind, and never communicate, as from yourself, or any one else, a sentiment of the like nature."

That settled the king-making idea. Never again did a man dare, by such a proposition, to assail the honor or misjudge the patriotism of George Washington.

To me, boys and girls, that instant of surprising temptation, righteous anger, and indignant reply marks one of the greatest moments in the life of America's greatest man–"the only man, in fact," so Lord Brougham, the Englishman declared, "upon whom the epithet 'great' so thoughtlessly lavished by men, may be justly bestowed."

Adapting for Families:

Principle: We have more freedom when our government is divided into groups that keep an eye on each other.

Simple Explanation: Only a king makes laws, carries out laws and then judges those laws. Kings usually don't rule fairly over the people because they are in charge of all three powers of government. In America, the three powers of government are split up between three different groups. One group makes laws, which is called the legislative branch of government. A different group carries out the laws, which is called the executive branch of government. Another group judges the law, which is called the judicial branch of government. That way the three different groups can check up on each other to make sure the government's powers aren't being used to rule unfairly over the people.

Discussion Questions:

1. What would happen in our home if only one person made all the rules and decided whether or not those rules were fair?
2. Would there ever be a time when it would be good for just one individual to make all laws, carry out all laws and judge all cases against the law? Why or why not?

See page 91 in the appendix for more references and quotes about Checks and Balances.

Principle 3
ACTIVELY ENGAGED

Freedom is best preserved when men form government that responds to those who are actively engaged in supporting and defending it.

EXPLANATION:

Although God created all men to be free, the great paradox is that freedom is not the natural state of man when he is not focused on maintaining and supporting that freedom. The Republican system of self-government our Founding Fathers—and God—gave to us requires that we, the people, act to preserve our freedom. Those who vote, advocate for issues, contact representatives, run for public office and serve in volunteer capacities, are those who are participating in the process of self-government and those who are defining what type of government we will live under. If we don't participate in the process of self-government, then we will find that the freedom we had expected to be handed down to us looks much more like oppression. No system of government can guarantee freedom will be perpetuated. All that a good system of government can guarantee is that the people themselves will get what they ultimately desire, sacrifice for, and deserve.

FROM THE CONSTITUTION:

"The House of Representatives shall be composed of Members chosen every second Year by the People of the several States."

Article I, Section 2, Clause 1

FROM THE FOUNDING FATHERS:

"These are the times that try men's souls. The summer-soldier and the sun-shine patriot will, in this crisis, shrink from the service of their country; but he that stands by it now, deserves the love and thanks of man and woman. Tyranny, like hell, is not easily conquered; yet we have this consolation with us, that the harder the conflict, the more glorious the triumph. What we obtain too cheap, we esteem too lightly: it is dearness only that gives every thing its value. Heaven knows how to put a proper price upon its goods; and it would be strange indeed if so celestial an article as FREEDOM should not be highly rated... Those who expect to reap the blessings of freedom must, like men, undergo the fatigue of supporting it"

Thomas Paine[1]

From the Prophets:

"We desperately need moral men and women who stand on principle, to be involved in the political process. Otherwise, we abdicate power to those whose designs are almost entirely selfish."

Gordon B. Hinckley[2]

From the Scriptures:

"For behold, it is not meet that I should command in all things; for he that is compelled in all things, the same is a slothful and not a wise servant; wherefore he receiveth no reward. Verily I say, men should be anxiously engaged in a good cause, and do many things of their own free will, and bring to pass much righteousness; For the power is in them, wherein they are agents unto themselves. And inasmuch as men do good they shall in nowise lose their reward."

Doctrine and Covenants 58:26-28

Story to Illustrate the Principle:

Two Obscure Heroes

From: George C. Eggleston, *Strange Stories from History for Young People* (Library of Alexandria, 2009).
Original grammar and spelling maintained.

When the British marched up from Savannah and took Charleston, in the spring of 1780, they thought the Revolution was at an end in the Southern States, and it really seemed so. Even the patriots thought it was useless to resist any longer, and so when the British ordered all the people to come together at different places and enrol themselves as British subjects, most of them were ready to do it, simply because they

1 Thomas Paine, *The American Crisis* (London: R. Carlile, 1819) 11, 63
2 Gordon B. Hinckley, *Stand a Little Taller* (Eagle Gate, 2001) 15

thought they could not help themselves.

Only a few daring men here and there were bold enough to think of refusing, and but for them the British could have set up the royal power again in South Carolina, and then they would have been free to take their whole force against the patriots farther north. The fate of the whole country depended, to a large extent, upon the courage of the few men who would not give up even at such a time, but kept up the fight against all odds. These brave men forced the British to keep an army in the South which they needed farther north.

The credit of beginning this kind of partisan warfare belongs chiefly to two or three plain men, who did it simply because they loved their country more than their ease.

The man who first began it was Justice Gaston–a white-haired patriot who lived on a little stream called Fishing Creek, near Rocky Mount. He was eighty years of age, and might well have thought himself too old to care about war matters; but he was a brave man and a patriot, and the people who lived near him were in the habit of taking his advice and doing as he did.

When the news came that Tarleton had killed a band of patriots under Colonel Buford in cold blood, Justice Gaston called his nine sons and many of his nephews around him. Joining hands, these young men promised each other that they never would take the British oath, and never would give up the cause, come what might.

Soon afterwards a British force came to the neighborhood, and all the people were ordered to meet at Rocky Mount to enrol their names and take the oath. One of the British officers went to see Justice Gaston, and tried to persuade him that it was folly to refuse. He knew that if Gaston advised the people to give up, there would be no trouble; but the white-haired patriot told him to his face that he would never take the oath himself or advise anybody else to do so.

As soon as the officer left the old man sent for his friends, and about thirty brave fellows met at his house that night, with their rifles in their hands. They knew there would be a strong force of British and Tories at Rocky Mount the next day, but, in spite of the odds against them, they made up their minds to attack the place, and when the time came they did so. Creeping through the woods, they suddenly came upon the crowd, and after a sharp fight sent the British flying helter-skelter in every direction. This stopped the work of enrolling the people as British subjects, and it did more than that. It showed the patriots through the whole country that they could still give the British a great deal of trouble, and after this affair many of the men who had thought of giving up rubbed up their rifles instead, and formed little bands of fighting men to keep the war going.

Adapting for Families:

Principle: We are most free when we are involved in our government.

Simple Explanation: In America, our government is only as good as our people. If good people aren't involved in government, then our government will be run by people who will destroy our freedom.

Discussion Questions:

1. What are some of the things we can do today to be involved in supporting and defending our freedom?
2. If we choose to not get involved with our government, but let only those who love power and authority be involved, what effect could this have on ourselves and on our government?
3. Have you seen an example of one person making a big difference?

See page 83 in the appendix for more references and quotes about being Actively Engaged.

Principle 4
LIMITED POWER

Freedom is best preserved when men form government to have its power limited by the people.

EXPLANATION:

As Lord Acton famously said, "Power tends to corrupt, and absolute power corrupts absolutely." Since governmental power is the power to act with force upon others, such authorization of force should be limited and narrowly defined. Government does not have a life of its own; it was created by man by virtue of his God-given rights and responsibilities for the purpose of serving man. It is therefore limited to do only those things which man himself can do but then authorizes government to do on his behalf. For instance, since each individual is endowed with the natural right to use force to protect his property against theft, individuals can organize a police force and delegate to them the power to protect their property. But since an individual doesn't have the natural right to use force to take someone else's property from him for his own benefit, individuals cannot organize government and delegate to them the power to take property from one in order to give to another.

FROM THE CONSTITUTION:

"Deriving their just powers from the consent of the governed" *(Source of power – 'the governed'. Use of power – 'consent')*

Declaration of Independence

FROM THE FOUNDING FATHERS:

"...It would be a dangerous delusion were a confidence in the men of our choice to silence our fears for the safety of our rights: that confidence is everywhere the parent of despotism: free government is founded in jealousy and not in confidence; it is jealousy and not confidence which prescribes limited Constitutions to bind down those whom we are obliged to trust with power: that our Constitution has accordingly fixed the limits to which and no further our confidence may go; . . . In questions of power then let no more be heard of confidence in man, but bind him down from mischief by the chains of the Constitution."

Thomas Jefferson[1]

From the Prophets:

"Since God created man with certain unalienable rights, and man, in turn, created government to help secure and safeguard those rights, it follows that man is superior to the creature which he created. Man is superior to government and should remain master over it, not the other way around."

Ezra Taft Benson[2]

From the Scriptures:

"That the civil magistrate should restrain crime, *but never control conscience*; should punish guilt, but *never suppress the freedom of the soul…* all governments have a right to enact such laws as in their own judgments are best calculated to secure the public interest; at the same time, however, *holding sacred the freedom of conscience.* We believe that every man should be honored in his station, rulers and magistrates as such, *being placed for the protection of the innocent and the punishment of the guilty.*"

Doctrine and Covenants 134:4-6 *(emphasis added)*

Story to Illustrate the Principle:

James Otis and How He Breathed Life into the Fight against Tyranny

From: Elbridge S. Brooks, *Historic Americans* (New York: Thomas Y. Crowell & Co., 1899), 34-45, abridged.
Original grammar and spelling maintained.

It was a raw February day in Boston town, and Mr. James Otis,

1 Ethelbert Dudley Warfield, A.M. LL. B., *The Kentucky Resolutions of 1798* (New York: The Knickerbocker Press 1887), 83.
2 Ezra T. Benson, *The Proper Role of Government* (1968).

advocate-general of the Colony of Massachusetts, buttoned his brown surtout closely about him, as he passed out through the round-topped doorway of his house on Court Street and walked briskly on toward the Royal Exchange tavern, or Stone's, –as the tavern was called "for short,"–on State Street. It was at Stone's that the lawyers and politicians of old Boston met to talk things over before court was opened in the State House across the way.

But though the day was raw the sturdy advocate-general did not feel nearly so much the sharp sea-turn that came in from the bay, damp and penetrating, as he did the responsibility that was laid upon him and the pinch of the struggle between duty and inclination. For Mr. Paxton, collector of customs for the king in Boston town, had determined to put a stop to the "tax-dodging" of those merchants of Massachusetts who denied the king's right to collect such duties, and who smuggled or secreted goods in their own houses in order to avoid the dues. Under the laws made for the colony, in England, such places could be searched and, if resistance were made, the officers, under the authority of a paper called a Writ of Assistance, could request or compel any citizen to assist them in their forcible search of a private house.

This law enraged the good people of the Bay Colony, but Mr. Paxton, the collector, was determined to force his order through, and he had petitioned the Supreme Court, sitting in Boston, to grant these writs of assistance. It was the duty of the advocate-general to argue such a case as this before the court and secure the writ. So Mr. Paxton called upon Mr. James Otis, as advocate-general, to argue the case for the crown.

But Mr. James Otis, the advocate-general, did not wish to do his official duty. He did not believe in the right of king or council to make such a law.

"A man's house is his castle," he declared, "and while he is quiet he is as well guarded as a prince. If these writs of assistance are made legal no man is safe–the privilege of safety at home is annihilated. Officers may enter our houses whenever they please and we cannot resist them. It is wrong; it is totally wrong. No act of Parliament can make such a writ stand. I cannot–I will not be party to it."

James Otis was an impulsive man, of quick temper and of hasty speech, but he was a lover of right and justice and liberty. When he made up his mind, however, he was quick to act, and before the short walk between his house and "Stone's" was over he had determined upon his course. He would refuse to argue the writ.

"But as judge-advocate you must argue it," said his friend Mr. Thacher, great lawyer and true patriot. "Your argument is right. The writ is not legal. Even what is binding in England cannot be used against us in America. But that is not for you to say. As advocate-general for the crown you must argue for the benefit of the crown; there is no other way."

"But there is a way, Thacher!" cried James Otis, turning on his friend. "It is the way of every honest man out of a dishonest situation. Here, Master Stone" he demanded in his impulsive way, and the landlord of the "ordinary" hurried up to answer Mr. Otis's summons; "some paper and a quill, quickly, please!"

Then seated at a table in a quiet corner, while Mr. Thacher stood beside him, James Otis dashed off a few hasty lines and showed the letter to his friend.

"That's the way I can fix it," said he.

It was the resignation of James Otis as advocate-general of the colony. It meant the loss of much practice, for which the crown paid good fees, but in the eyes of James Otis loss of money was not to be compared with loss of honor.

No sooner was the fact of this resignation known than the merchants of Salem and Boston, the two ports most affected by this odious search law, applied to James Otis to take their case and argue against the writ.

It would be before this very court, in which, as advocate-general, it would have been his duty to argue in behalf of the writ, and the opportunity was one which his impulsive nature could not resist.

"I shall be glad to do it, gentlemen," he said to those who sought his aid; but when they offered liberal fees in payment of his services Otis was as quick tempered as he had been with his friend Thacher.

"Fees?" he cried, "fees, do you say? In such a case, gentlemen,

I despise all fees," and he would take none; for, in this case, resistance to what he considered tyranny was duty, and not a matter of business.

This feeling grew within him as the time of the trial approached, and when, on a late day in that same month of February, 1761, he entered the courtroom in the Old State House on State Street, where the writ was to be argued, he was so inspired by his theme that he made one of the famous speeches of the world.

The courtroom–they still show it to visitors, in the east end of the famous Old State House, preserved as a memorial of patriotism by Boston town–was filled with lawyers and interested listeners as Otis rose to speak, for the case was one that affected the safety and manhood of every citizen of the Bay State. Down upon this opponent of kingly prerogative looked the full-length portraits of Charles and James, kings of England both, who held to that ridiculous theory that "the king can do no wrong." Five judges in scarlet robes, wide bands, and mighty wigs, sat to hear the case, and central among them as chief-justice was Thomas Hutchinson, who combined in his single person the lucrative offices of lieutenant-governor of Massachusetts, chief-justice of the Superior Court of the colony, governor of the castle, member of the council, and judge of probate. Mr. Thacher, the friend and associate of Otis, had just completed an able, but mild and moderate speech when the "champion of the people" sprang to his feet.

Already he was tingling with his theme; at once he burst into an indignant protest against the drag the king would place on liberty.

"I take this opportunity to declare," Otis burst forth, "that, to my dying day, I will oppose with all the faculties God has given me, all such instruments of slavery on the one hand, and villany on the other, as this writ of assistance."

This stirred the people. One young man, who later became a great factor in America's independence and progress, John Adams, of Quincy, was so aroused and electrified by the words he heard that, fifty-seven years after, he could repeat almost word for word the speech of Otis–a speech that so aroused and awakened his patriotism that, as his grandson declared, "that speech of Otis was to Adams like the oath of Hamilcar administered to Hannibal." It made of the young man an instant patriot.

"I was solicited," continued Otis, "to argue this cause as advocate-general; and because I would not, I have been charged with desertion of my office. To this charge I can give a very sufficient answer: I renounced that office, and I argue this cause from the same principle . . . . It is in opposition to a kind of power the exercise of which in former periods of English history" (here he glanced significantly to the two royal portraits on the wall) "cost one king of England his head and another his throne... I cheerfully submit myself to every odious name for conscience' sake; and from my soul I despise all those whose guilt, malice, or folly has made them my foes. Let the consequences be what they will, I am determined to proceed. The only principles of public conduct that are worthy of a gentleman or a man are to sacrifice estate, ease, health, applause, and even life, to the sacred call of his country."

Then he went deeply into the case and for four hours the speech went on. Into it James Otis put all the strength of his mind, all the force of his indignation, all the splendor of his eloquence, all the brilliancy of his magnetic power.

Parliament, he said, could not legalize tyranny. "Though it should be made in the very words of the petition," he declared, "It would be void, for every act against the Constitution is void."

"Every man," he declared, "is individually independent. His right to his life, his liberty, and his property no created being can rightfully contest; these rights are inherent and inalienable."

It was just such language as this that, years after, opened the Declaration of Independence, which James Otis thus inspired.

Individuals, he said, when associated together as a nation for mutual protection and defence did not surrender their natural rights. "Our ancestors, as British subjects," he said, "and we their descendants, as British subjects, were entitled to all those rights, and we are not to be cheated out of them by a phantom of virtual representation or any other fiction of law and politics."

Then Otis explained what taxes were, when they were just, and laid down the doctrine that brought on the American Revolution. "Taxation without representation is tyranny." Acts imposing unjust or oppressive taxation, he declared, were tyrannical, and never had and never could be executed in America. "If the king of Great Britain, in person," he declared, "were encamped on Boston Common at the head of twenty thousand men, with all his navy on our coast, he would not be able to execute those laws. They would be resisted or eluded."

He grew bolder and more impassioned as he concluded. He denounced the taxation and revenue laws of England, "Made by a foreign legislature without our consent, by a legislature which has no feeling for us and whose interest prompts them to tax us to the quick." Then he went on reproaching the British nation, Parliament, and king with injustice, illiberality, ingratitude, and oppression in their conduct toward the people of America, in a style of oratory, so John Adams reported, "that I have never heard equaled in this or any country."

The grounds that James Otis took and the sentiments he uttered in that famous five-hour speech do not sound strange to us. We have been brought up to believe in personal liberty, no taxation without representation, and the security of house and home; we have no need for such impassioned appeals or such attacks on royalty. We have no fear of royalty today, and we have a way of speaking our minds if things do not go to suit us in matters of state. But in that day it was treason to criticize; it was crime to talk of liberty; and the words of Otis came like a strong wind blowing down from the heights of freedom.

"I do say in the most solemn manner," John Adams declared fifty years later, "that Mr. Otis's oration against writs of assistance breathed into this nation the breath of life."

It set people thinking; it gave them courage; it put into expression that feeling that something was wrong in the acts of Great Britain, which, later, took definite shape at Lexington and Concord, and burst into the protest of freemen in the Declaration of Independence.

"This was the opening scene of American resistance," John Adams wrote to a friend. "It began in New England and made its first battle-ground in a court-room. A lawyer of Boston, with a tongue of flame and the inspiration of a seer, stepped forward to demonstrate that all arbitrary authority was unconstitutional and against the law. Then and there, in that court-room, the child Independence was born."

The judges were against him and their decision was adverse; but the writs were not issued publicly. The people were aroused, and the seeds planted by the words of Otis in time burst forth, grew and blossomed into a righteous and successful resistance to tyranny. His speech made patriots, and those patriots in time made America free.

ADAPTING FOR FAMILIES:

Principle: We have more freedom when government can't do whatever it wants.

Explanation: The people made the government and gave the government power to do things for us. Government is supposed to only do what we ask them to do. If government starts doing things we don't ask them to do, or starts telling us what to do, then that makes us less free.

DISCUSSION QUESTIONS:

1. Is it right for one person to have control over another person?
2. Are people in charge of government or is government in charge of people? Explain.
3. How does Doctrine and Covenants 121:39 relate to the principle of limiting governmental power?

See page 131 in the appendix for more references and quotes about Limited Power.

Principle 5
INDIVIDUAL AGENCY

Freedom is best preserved when men form government to respect individual choice and accountability as foundational to man's underlying purpose and reason for existence.

EXPLANATION:

In order to govern one's self—which is the very purpose of our life here on earth—one must have a knowledge of good and evil, must have the ability to choose between right and wrong, must know and experience the consequences associated with those choices, and must experience opposition that tempts him to choose evil over good. Having laws that permit individuals to fully participate in exercising their agency allows them to experience the full breadth and depth of their mortal life. Governments that force their citizens to act a certain way inevitably infringe on these elements of self-government. This ultimately leads to a reduction in agency and a frustration of the purpose of life here on earth.

FROM THE CONSTITUTION:

"The enumeration in the Constitution, of certain rights, shall not be construed to deny or disparage others retained by the people."

9th Amendment

FROM THE FOUNDING FATHERS:

"It is evident that no other form [of government] would be reconcilable with the genius of the people of America; with the fundamental principles of the Revolution; or with that honorable determination which animates every votary of freedom, to rest all our political experiments on the capacity of mankind for self-government."

James Madison[1]

1 Publius [pseud.], *The Federalist Papers* (1787) Federalist Paper No. 39.

FROM THE PROPHETS:

"The two most important documents affecting the destiny of America are the Declaration of Independence and the Constitution of the United States. Both these immortal papers related primarily to the freedom of the individual."

David O. McKay[2]

FROM THE SCRIPTURES:

"According to the laws and constitution of the people, which I have suffered to be established, and should be maintained for the rights and protection of all flesh, according to just and holy principles; *That every man may act in doctrine and principle pertaining to futurity, according to the moral agency which I have given unto him, that every man may be accountable for his own sins in the day of judgment. Therefore, it is not right that any man should be in bondage one to another. And for this purpose have I established the Constitution of this land*, by the hands of wise men whom I have raised up unto this very purpose, and redeemed the land by the shedding of blood."

Doctrine and Covenants 101:77-80 *(emphasis added)*

STORY TO ILLUSTRATE THE PRINCIPLE:

Patrick Henry: Give Me Liberty or Give Me Death

From: Elbridge S. Brooks, *Historic Americans* (New York: Thomas Y. Crowell & Co., 1899), 73-85, abridged.
Original grammar and spelling maintained.

St. John's Church in Richmond is a plain and unpretending little church as it stands almost on the summit of one of Richmond's sightly hills,–Church hill, it is called,– at the corner of Broadway and Twenty-fourth Street. Small as it is, the church today is much larger than it was on that day in 1775–Thursday, the twenty-third of March–when, rising to his feet, in the pew still shown to visitors and marked by a memorial tablet, Patrick Henry threw down the gauntlet to King George and declared war on the haughty prerogative of Great Britain.

The second Revolutionary convention of Virginia was assem-

2 David O. Mckay, *Favorable and Unfavorable Phases of Present-day Conditions* (The Ensign, April 1952) 11.

bled in that old church on the hill in Richmond. The first convention had met at Williamsburg the year before. And now the second Revolutionary congress of Virginia had met to debate upon the question whether Virginia should declare for peace or war. Everywhere, throughout the colonies, the people were restless; everywhere there was talk of resistance, and from Massachusetts Bay to Charleston harbor the local military companies were being organized for possible emergencies, and drilled to the use of arms. But prudence was keeping men back from act or speech that might be deemed aggressive; prudence was still holding men loyal to the king.

So, when the question of arming the militia of Virginia came up in the colonial convention, and Patrick Henry introduced a resolution "that this colony be immediately put into a posture of defence and a committee be appointed to prepare a plan for embodying, arming, and disciplining such a number of men as may be sufficient for that purpose," prudence interfered to prevent so menacing a move.

"The resolution is premature," objected some of the more conservative members. "War with Great Britain may come," they said; "but it may be prevented."

"May come?" exclaimed Patrick Henry; "may come? It has come!" And then, rising in his place, in that narrow pew in old St. John's, he broke out into that famous speech which now "fills so great a space in the traditions of Revolutionary eloquence."

Tall and thin in figure, with stooping shoulders and sallow face, carelessly dressed in his suit of "parson's gray," Patrick Henry faced the president of the convention and began calmly, courteously, and with dignity.

"No man, Mr. President," he said, "thinks more highly than I do of the patriotism as well as the abilities of the very honorable gentlemen who have just addressed the house. But different men often see the same subject in different lights; and, therefore, I hope it will not be thought disrespectful to those gentlemen if, entertaining as I do opinions of a character very opposite to theirs, I should speak forth my sentiments freely and without reserve."

Then he flung aside courtesy and calmness. "This is no time for ceremony," he told them hotly. "The question before the house is one of awful moment to the country. For my own part, I consider it as nothing less than a question of freedom or slavery . . . .

"Should I keep back my opinions at such a time, through fear of giving offence, I should consider myself," he declared impressively, "as guilty of treason toward my country, and of an act of disloyalty to the majesty of Heaven, which I revere above all earthly kings."

Then he began his argument with that sentence which is still a household word in the mouths of men: "Mr. President, it is natural for man to indulge in the illusions of hope;" and, showing how under existing circumstances hope was but a false beacon, and experience was the only safe guide, he called attention to the armament of England, and demanded, "I ask gentlemen, sir, what means this martial array, if its purpose be not to force us to submission?"

Impressively he showed them that England's display of might was meant for America, "sent over to bind and rivet upon us those chains which the British ministry have been so long forging."

He demanded how his associates intended to oppose this British tyranny. Argument had failed, entreaty and supplication were of no avail, compromise was exhausted; petitions and remonstrances, supplications and prostrations, were alike disregarded – "we have been spurned with contempt from the foot of the throne," he said.

"There is no longer," he declared, "any room for hope. If we wish to be free....if we wish not basely to abandon the noble struggle in which we have been so long engaged," he paused, and then, as one of his hearers said, with all the calm dignity of Cato addressing the Senate; like a "voice from heaven uttering the doom of fate," he added solemnly but decisively, –"we must fight! I repeat it, sir, we must fight! An appeal to arms and to the God of hosts is all that is left to us."

Then, his calmness all gone, his voice deepening and his slender form swayed with the passion of his own determination, he flung himself into that fervent appeal for union in resistance that we all know so well:

"Besides, sir, we shall not fight our battles alone. There is a just God who presides over the destinies of nations, who will raise up friends to fight our battles for us. The battle, sir, is not to the strong alone; it is to the vigilant, the active, the brave . . . It is now too late to retire from the contest. There is no retreat now but in submission and slavery. Our chains are forged. Their clanking may be heard on the plains of Boston. The war is inevitable; and let it come. I repeat it, sir,–let it come!"

Can you not almost hear that wonderful voice as it makes that terrible invitation with all the force of confident faith and repressed enthusiasm? Can you not almost see that swaying form, those forcible gestures, that face stern with purpose? Old men there were, years after its utterance, who could not forget that tremendous speech nor how, with their eyes riveted on the speaker, they sat, as one of them expressed it, "sick with excitement."

And then came the ending – one of those immortal bursts of eloquence, a fitting climax to what had come before:

"It is vain, sir, to extenuate the matter. Gentlemen may cry, Peace, peace, but there is no peace! The war is actually begun. The next gale that sweeps from the north will bring to our ears the clash of resounding arms. Our brethren are already in the field. Why stand we here idle? What is it that gentlemen wish? What would they have? Is life so dear, or peace so sweet, as to be purchased at the price of chains and slavery? Forbid it, Almighty God! I know not what course others may take, but as for me give me liberty or give me death!"

That wonderful speech has lived in men's memories and hearts for far over 200 years. For other hundreds it will live as one of the trumpet calls leading men to fight for freedom or to die free men. That speech has made Patrick Henry live forever as America's impassioned orator; but better still, it turned Virginia, as in a flash, for independence, and made her stand side by side with Massachusetts, leaders and coworkers in the fight for liberty.

How ready Patrick Henry was to live up to his grand principles of liberty or death we may discover in his story. From the convention he went speedily to the field. He was made commander-in-chief of Virginia's Revolutionary army, as George Washington was of the

Continental forces, and almost the first overt act of the war in Virginia, so Thomas Jefferson declared, was committed by Patrick Henry.

Adapting for Families:

Principle: We have more freedom when we get to make choices for ourselves rather than government making choices for us.

Simple Explanation: Heavenly Father sent us here on earth to makes choices. When we make good choices we are happy. When we make bad choices we are sad. We learn from our choices. If government makes choices for us then we don't get to learn from our choices what is good and what is bad.

Discussion Questions:

1. What would it be like to live in a country where you weren't allowed to choose?
2. The war in heaven was about agency. How is that battle still going on in government today?
3. How does my self-government affect our family's government and our nation's government?

See page 123 in the appendix for more references and quotes about Individual Agency.

Principle 6

FEDERALISM

Freedom is best preserved when men form government to operate as close to the people as possible.

EXPLANATION:

There are different levels of government. The most basic level is self-government, which is based on each individual exercising and defending his God-given rights. Other levels of government–municipal, county, state and federal–are derived from the individual's rights and his delegation of those rights, therefore governmental actions should be performed by the level closest to the individual. The only time a more distant level of government should be tasked with performing a function is if the level closer to the people is incompetent to do so.

CONSTITUTIONAL REFERENCE:

"The powers not delegated to the United States by the Constitution, nor prohibited by it to the States, are reserved to the States respectively, or to the people."

10th Amendment

FROM THE FOUNDING FATHERS:

"Let the national government be entrusted with the defence of the nation, and its foreign and federal relations; the State governments with the civil rights, laws, police, and administration of what concerns the State generally; the counties with the local concerns of the counties, and each ward direct the interests within itself. . . the secret will be found to be in the making himself the depository of the powers respecting himself, so far as he is competent to them, and delegating only what is beyond his competence... to higher and higher orders."

Thomas Jefferson[1]

---

1 Philip B. Kurland and Ralph Lerner, Ed., *The Founders' Constitution*, (Chicago: University of Chicago Press) 14: 421—23

FROM THE PROPHETS:

There appears to me to be a trend to shift responsibility for life and its processes from the individual to the state. In this shift there is a basic violation of the law of the harvest, or the law of justice. The attitude of 'something for nothing' is encouraged. The government is often looked to as the source of wealth. There is a feeling that the government should step in and take care of one's needs, one's emergencies, and one's future… When the responsibility for their own welfare is completely shifted from the shoulders of individuals and families to the state, a lethal blow is struck at both the roots of our prosperity and our moral growth."

Howard W. Hunter[2]

FROM THE SCRIPTURES:

"Moreover thou shalt provide out of all the people able men, such as fear God, men of truth, hating covetousness; and place such over them, to be rulers of thousands, and rulers of hundreds, rulers of fifties, and rulers of tens. And let them judge the people at all seasons: and it shall be, that every great matter they shall bring unto thee, but every small matter they shall judge; so shall it be easier for thyself, and *they shall bear the burden with thee*."

Exodus 18:21-22 *(emphasis added)*

STORY TO ILLUSTRATE THE PRINCIPLE:

An Anecdote of Washington

Mara L. Pratt, *American History Stories You Never Read in School but Should Have* (Randall Company, 1993), 88.
Original grammar and spelling maintained.

During the revolution, George Washington was one day riding by a group of soldiers who did not know him. They were busily engaged in raising a beam to the top of some military works. It was a difficult task, and often the corporal's voice could be heard shouting, "Now you have it!" "All ready! Pull!"

Washington quietly asked the corporal why he didn't turn to and help them. "Sir," angrily replied the corporal, "Do you realize that I am the corporal?"

2 Hunter, Howard W. 1966. *"The Law of the Harvest"* (speech). Text transcript from Latter-day Conservative. http://latterdayconservative.com/howard-w-hunter/the-law-of-the-harvest/

Washington politely raised his hat, saying, "I did not realize it. Beg pardon Mr. Corporal"

Then dismounting, he himself fell to work and helped the men til the beam was raised. Before leaving he turned to the corporal, and, wiping the perspiration from his face, said, "If ever you need assistance like this again, call upon Washington, your commander-in-chief, and I will come."

The confused corporal turned red, then white, as he realized that this was Washington himself to whom he had been so pompous; and we hope he learned a lesson of true greatness.

ADAPTING FOR FAMILIES:

Principle: We have more freedom when we do for ourselves all that we can do and ask the level of government closest to us to help when we need it.

Simple Explanation: People should do what they can for themselves. If they can't do something for themselves, then they should ask the closest level of government for help, which is local government. If local government cannot help, then the next level (the state government) should be asked. If the state government cannot help, then the next level (national government) should be asked. We give our freedom away when we give unnecessary responsibilities to levels of government far away from us.

DISCUSSION QUESTIONS:

1. Why does Heavenly Father want us to do as much as we can for ourselves and not have government do it for us?
2. What are some similarities and differences between church government (prophets and apostles, stake presidents, bishops, families) and our nation's government (federal, state, county, local). (Helpful point: Consider that in the Church, Jesus Christ has authority that flows down. In America, the people have authority that flows up.)

See page 95 in the appendix for more references and quotes about Federalism

Principle 7

God's Central Role

Freedom is best preserved when men form a government which places God and His laws as supreme.

Explanation:

Since governments create laws that define right and wrong actions, then all systems of government must be based on a moral code. No amount of laws can make men moral, but good laws are formed on moral and religious principles that also comply with God's laws. When this occurs, governments flourish. For instance, God created all men to be equal in His eyes. When a system of government likewise recognizes that all men are equal under its law, such a system complies with God's truth and yields the maximum amount of freedom for those who live under it. However, even with such abundant freedom, only a deeply held conviction of the existence of God and His truths by the general population will provide a truly functional and sustainably free government, because the people will govern themselves out of respect for higher laws—God's.

From the Constitution:

"To assume among the powers of the earth, the separate and equal station to which the Laws of Nature and of Nature's God entitle them...We hold these truths to be self-evident, that all men are created equal, that they are endowed by their Creator with certain unalienable Rights, that among these are Life, Liberty and the pursuit of Happiness. . . . appealing to the Supreme Judge of the world for the rectitude of our intentions . . . with a firm reliance on the protection of divine Providence, we mutually pledge to each other our Lives, our Fortunes and our sacred Honor." *(Notice the three governmental functions that place God as the great lawgiver and Creator, the Supreme Judge, and the Omnipotent protector).*

The Declaration of Independence

From the Founding Fathers:

"We have no government armed with power capable of contending with human passions unbridled by morality and religion. Avarice, ambition, revenge, or gallantry would break the strongest cords of our Constitution, as a whale goes through a net. Our Constitution was made only for a moral and religious people. It is wholly inadequate to the government of any other."

John Adams[1]

From the Prophets:

"To serve God, and keep His commandments are first and foremost with me. If this is higher law, so be it. As it is with me, so should it be with every department of the government; for this doctrine is based upon the principles of virtue, and integrity; with it the Government, her Constitution, and free institutions are safe; without it no power can evert their speedy destruction. It is the life-giving power to the government; it is the vital element on which she exists and prospers; in its absence she sinks to rise no more."

Brigham Young[2]

From the Scriptures:

"We believe that governments were instituted of God for the benefit of man; and that he holds men accountable for their acts in relation to them, both in making laws and administering them, for the good and safety of society. . . human laws being instituted for the express purpose of regulating our interests as individuals and nations, between man and man; and divine laws given of heaven, prescribing rules on spiritual concerns, for faith and worship, both to be answered by man to his Maker."

Doctrine and Covenants 134:1, 6

1 Charles Francis Adams, *The Works of John Adams, Second President of the United States* (Boston: Little, Brown and Company, 1854) 229
2 G.D. Watt, *Journal of Discourses by President Brigham Young* (Liverpool: F. D. Richards), 176.

Story to Illustrate the Principle:

Benjamin Franklin Calls for Prayer at the Constitutional Convention

Max Farrand, Ed., *The Records of the Federal Convention of 1787, Vol. III,* (New Haven: Yale University Press, 1911).
Original grammar and spelling maintained.

The Constitutional Convention had been meeting for over a month and was facing the very real probability that the convention would disband over various heated issues – including the debate about representation in the federal legislature. It was with this tension and apprehension in the air that Benjamin Franklin, 81 years of age, rose to address the body. According to James Madison's notes, here is what he said:

"Mr. President, the small progress we have made after 4 or five weeks close attendance & continual reasonings with each other-our different sentiments on almost every question, several of the last producing as many noes as ays, is methinks a melancholy proof of the imperfection of the Human Understanding. We indeed seem to feel our own want of political wisdom, since we have been running about in search of it. We have gone back to ancient history for models of Government, and examined the different forms of those Republics which having been formed with the seeds of their own dissolution now no longer exist. And we have viewed Modern States all round Europe, but find none of their Constitutions suitable to our circumstances.

In this situation of this Assembly, groping as it were in the dark to find political truth, and scarce able to distinguish it when presented to us, how has it happened, Sir, that we have not hitherto once thought of humbly applying to the Father of lights to illuminate our understandings? In the beginning of the Contest with G. Britain, when we were sensible of danger we had daily prayer in this room for the divine protection. Our prayers, Sir, were heard, & they were graciously answered. All of us who were engaged in the struggle must have observed frequent instances of a superintending providence in our favor.

To that kind providence we owe this happy opportunity of consulting in peace on the means of establishing our future national felicity. And have we now forgotten that powerful friend? or do we imagine that we no longer need his assistance? I have lived, Sir, a long time, and the longer I live, the more convincing proofs I see of this truth- that God Governs in the affairs of men. And if a sparrow cannot fall to the ground without his notice, is it probable that an empire can rise without his aid? We have been assured, Sir, in the sacred writings, that "except the Lord build the House they labour in vain that build it." I firmly believe this; and I also believe that without his concurring aid we shall succeed in this political building no better, than the Builders of Babel: We shall be divided by our little partial local interests; our projects will be confounded, and we ourselves shall become a reproach and bye word down to future ages. And what is worse, mankind may hereafter from this unfortunate instance, despair of establishing Governments by Human wisdom and leave it to chance, war and conquest.

I therefore beg leave to move-that henceforth prayers imploring the assistance of Heaven, and its blessings on our deliberations, be held in this Assembly every morning before we proceed to business."

Adapting for Families:

Principle: We have more freedom when government respects and loves Heavenly Father.

Simple Explanation: If a people and their representatives turn to Heavenly Father and keep His commandments, then they will have peace that Heavenly Father will take care of them. If not, they suffer sad consequences of their own bad choices that make them less and less free.

Discussion Questions:

1. What scripture stories show what happens when people don't remember God?

2. What can happen to a nation and to its people when what is legal is not moral?

See page 113 in the appendix for more references and quotes about God's Central Role in government

Principle 8
Republican Government

Freedom is best preserved when men form a representative government to operate under the rule of law as determined by the voice of the people.

Explanation:

God is a God of order. He governs the universe by laws – natural laws – that are eternal and fixed. Likewise, good government is based on laws, not on the changing opinions and whims of men. In the Republic of the United States, the Constitution serves as the supreme law of the land. It was written based on principles of freedom and on human nature, both of which do not change over time. Since the people are the ultimate sovereigns in a Republic, they get to choose representatives that then serve the public. However, these representatives are bound by oath, not to do the will of the people, but instead to uphold and defend the Constitution. It is the law itself that rules over the people and their representatives. No one is above the law. In a representative government the people are separated from direct governmental power which calms the passions of the masses and allows public servants the necessary time to fully deliberate and consider measures that aim to protect and preserve freedom for their constituents.

From the Constitution:

"The United States shall guarantee to every State in this union a Republican Form of Government."

Article IV, Section 4, Clause 1

From the Founding Fathers:

"It has been observed that a pure democracy if it were practicable would be the most perfect government. Experience has proved that no position is more false than this. The ancient democracies in which the people themselves deliberated never possessed one good feature of government. Their very character was tyranny; their figure deformity."

Alexander Hamilton[1]

FROM THE PROPHETS:

"My visits to underprivileged countries and among subjugated peoples who have placed their trust in governments of dominating men, rather than in governments of constitutional law, have shown me the importance and the great blessed privilege that is ours to live in this country where the basic law of the Constitution safeguards us in our God-given rights."

Harold B. Lee[2]

FROM THE SCRIPTURES:

"Therefore, I, the Lord, justify you, and your brethren of my church, in befriending that law which is the constitutional law of the land; And as pertaining to law of man, whatsoever is more or less than this, cometh of evil. I, the Lord God, make you free, therefore ye are free indeed; and *the law also maketh you free*. Nevertheless, when the wicked rule the people mourn. Wherefore, honest men and wise men should be sought for diligently, and good men and wise men ye should observe to uphold; otherwise whatsoever is less than these cometh of evil."

Doctrine and Covenants 98:6-10

STORY TO ILLUSTRATE THE PRINCIPLE:

Philip Brusque

William M. Giffin, *Civics for Young Americans* (New York: A. Lovell & Co., 1888).

Original grammar and spelling maintained.

Young Brusque was a Frenchman, who lived in France about

1 Hamilton, Alexander. 1788. "Urging Ratification of the Constitution" (speech). Text transcript from The Federalist Papers Project. https:// thefederalistpapers.org/founders/hamilton/alexander-hamilton-on-democracy-speech-in-new-york-urging-ratification-of-the-u-s-constitution-june-21-1788.

2 Harold B. Lee, *Ye Are the Light of the World* (Deseret Book Co. 1974) 232-33.

the year 1789, or at the time of the French Revolution. At the time of the Revolution, France was a monarchy, meaning they were ruled by a king.

In 1789 the common people of France determined to overthrow the government. Thousands of persons were executed by them. One of the most active of the people was young Brusque, who, with many others, thought that if the government could only be overthrown, he would be very happy. He thought that then he could do as he liked, without being restrained by any law, except the moral sense of man. He thought that laws were unfair, and that no man should have to be subject to them. In fact, Philip took such an active part that he soon found it unsafe for him to stay in Paris, and hence, with many others, he set sail for a foreign land. But alas! When but a few days out, a great storm arose and all on board were drowned, save Philip, who was washed ashore on a lone island, and what seemed to please him most of all was, that the island was without a single human inhabitant except himself.

When Philip found himself alone on the island, he was delighted, and exclaimed: "Now I shall be happy. Here I can enjoy perfect liberty. Here is no prison like the Bastille; here is no king to make slaves of his fellow-men; here is no Robespierre to plot the murder of his fellow-citizens. Liberty, how have I worshipped thee! And here on this lone island I have found thee. Here I can labor or rest, eat or drink, wake or sleep, as I please. Here is no one to control my actions or my thoughts. In my native country all the land belongs to a few persons; but here I can take as much land as I please. I can freely pick the fruit from the trees, according to my choice or my wants. How different is my situation from what it was in France! There, everything belongs to somebody, and I was restrained from taking anything, unless I paid for it. Here, all is free, all is mine. Here, I can enjoy perfect liberty. In France, I was under the check and control of a thousand laws; here, there is no law but my own will. Here, I have indeed found perfect freedom."

Philip, you see, was quite happy. Thus he continued for about a year, when he began to feel very lonely. How he longed to see a human being once more! Each day found him on the top of a high hill looking wishfully out at sea for a sail. One day while he was watching, he began to talk as follows: "Liberty is, indeed, a dear and beautiful thing; but still I want something beside liberty. I want to hear a human voice. I want to look into a human face. I want someone to speak to. I feel as if my very heart would wither for the want of a friend. I feel a thirst within, and I have no means of satisfying it. I feel within a voice speaking, and there is no answer. That beautiful island is becoming a desert to me, without even an echo. Dear France! Dear, dear home! How gladly would I give up this hollow and useless liberty for the pleasure of friendship and society! I would be willing to be restrained by the thousand meshes of the law, if I might once more enjoy the pleasure of living in the midst of my fellow-men."

Ah, my young friends, what a change had come over Philip in one short year! Short to us, but alas! How long, how very long, it had been to him. One day, on going to the top of the hill, Philip thought he saw something moving. It was about a mile from where he was standing, and looking sharply, he found that it was a human being. O, how his heart leaped for joy! He set off like a wild deer toward the stranger. When near enough, he saw it was a man. He ran right up to him with open arms. The man's name was Jacques Piquet. He was a fisherman from Mauritius. He had been out fishing, and the wind had blown him so far out to sea, that he could not get back to land. When he was about to give up all hopes, his small boat was dashed to pieces, and Jacques, being a good swimmer, saved his life by swimming to the island, which happened to be the one on which Philip was living.

How happy Philip was! He put his arms around the fisherman and kissed him again and again. He took the stranger and led him to his cave. Next he gathered some fresh pineapples and other fruit, and when he saw the fisherman eating them he clapped his hands in joy. Philip also ran to get Jacques some fresh water to drink. This was all very strange for Philip to do, as he was a proud fellow, and had he been compelled to serve the fisherman he would have hated and resisted the work but because he was doing it of his own free will and accord he found pleasure in it. Philip continued to wait on the fisherman for some little time. At last, however, there came a new order of things, and the fisherman began to order Philip to do this and that for him. This made Brusque very angry, and he told the fisherman he might wait on himself.

This, in turn, made Jacques angry, and soon from words they came to blows. Brusque, being the stronger of the two, dealt Jacques a blow on the head which felled him to the ground, where he lay without motion, seeming actually to be dead.

No sooner did Philip see the condition of the fisherman, that he thought to himself: "What a strange creature I am! A few weeks since I was made with joy at the arrival of this man; soon he became the tyrant of my life. I then wished him dead. I forgot that he had rights as well as myself. In taking his life I did a great wrong to justice, to liberty, and to myself."

While Brusque was thinking these thoughts, the fisherman moved and showed signs of returning life. Philip was again full of joy, and, fetching some water, sprinkled it over the man's face. He soon recovered, and Philip led him to the cave, where, lying down, he went to sleep. Again Philip fell to thinking.

"Jacques is alive again, and I am relieved of a load. When I was alone I was perfectly free, but I soon found that freedom without society was a sad condition of things. I therefore yearned for society, and I had it. But it soon became a torment to me. When, then, is the difficulty? I believe it is the want of some rules, by which we may regulate our conduct. Though there are but two of us, still we find it necessary to enter into a compact. We must form a government; we must submit to laws, rules and regulations. We must each submit to the abridgment of some portion of our liberty, some portion of our privileges in order to secure the rest."

Philip now returned to the cave, where he found the fisherman much better. Philip spoke to him of the necessity of laying down certain rules, by which the essential rights of each should be preserved and a state of harmony insured. To this Jacques agreed, and the following code of laws being drawn up by Philip, they were passed unanimously:

"Be it ordained by Philip Brusque, late of France, and Jacques Piquet, of Maritius, to insure harmony, establish justice, and promote the good of all parties:

1. This island shall be called Fredonia.

2. Liberty being a great good in itself, and the right of every human being, it shall only be abridged so far as the good of

society may require. But as all laws restrain liberty, we, the people of Fredonia, submit to the following:

3. The cave, called the Castaway's Home, lately occupied by Philip Brusque, shall be alternately occupied for a day and night by said Philip Brusque and Jacques Piquet, the former beginning this day, and the latter taking it the next day, and so forth.

4. Each person shall have a right to build himself a house, and shall have exclusive possession of the same.

5. If two persons wish the same fruit at the same time, they shall draw lots for the first choice, if they cannot agree otherwise as to the division.

6. If any difference arises between the two parties, Philip Brusque and Jacques Piquet, they shall decide such questions by lot.

7. This code of laws shall be changed, or modified, or added to, only by the consent of the parties, Philip Brusque and Jacques Piquet.

All which is done this 27th day of June, A.D. 18–

This was neatly cut with a penknife on a board which had come ashore from the wreck of Philip's vessel, and it became the statute law of the island of Fredonia.

From this story of Philip we learn that absolute liberty cannot be enjoyed except by an individual in solitude, where he has no contact with his fellow-men. From it we also learn that even supposing there are but two persons living together, some rules, or laws, by which they may regulate their conduct, become necessary. The truth is, my young friends, people cannot live together in society without government. Even two persons on an island find that, to prevent quarreling, they must define their mutual rights and privileges; or, in short, they must enact laws, and, as a matter of course, these laws are restraints upon natural or absolute liberty.

Thus it is that we are today living in a country governed by laws. And the best of all is, that our laws, like those of Philip and the fisherman, are our own; that is, they are made by us. And that is what makes our government one of the grandest in all the world.

ADAPTING FOR FAMILIES:

Principle: We have more freedom when we have a Constitution to guide us with laws made by our representatives.

Simple Explanation: In everything we do there are rules that we must follow so we can be happy. The Constitution helps us to know what the rules for government are. The laws are the rules that government and everyone else must follow so that the entire country can be peaceful and happy. The people that make the laws are chosen by us.

DISCUSSION QUESTIONS:

1. Why does our family have rules?
2. What would happen if our family didn't have rules?
3. How is our family government similar to or different than the Republican Government of our nation? (authority, accountability, representation, order, structure, etc.)

See page 149 in the appendix for more references and quotes about Republican Government

Principle 9
PRIVATE PROPERTY

Freedom is best preserved when men form government to recognize the ownership and control of private property as the basis for liberty.

EXPLANATION:

The plan of salvation revolves around ownership: owning our choices, our desires, our thoughts, and our motives. The personal ownership of property is central to the plan of salvation because it represents the tangible evidence of where we have chosen to apply our time, our talents and our energy–or in simpler terms, our agency. This makes private property an extension of who we are and, like our life and our liberty, it is therefore rightfully defended by use of force when we are threatened to be deprived of it.

We know that Heavenly Father has provided things to act and things to be acted upon (2 Nephi 2:14). When we use our agency to act upon the things of this world and thereby acquire property, the personal ownership of that property serves as the natural fruit of our labors. We are held accountable for how and why we obtain property and for what we do with it once it is ours, but if we don't own and control property, the purpose and value of our life and liberty is reduced. Without private property the motive to act would be diminished since the reward (property) of our efforts would be owned by someone else. And, our control over our life and liberty would be severely limited since it is property and its use that provides for the necessities of life.

FROM THE CONSTITUTION:

"No person shall be deprived of life, liberty or property without due process of law."

5th Amendment

FROM THE FOUNDING FATHERS:

"The moment the idea is admitted into society, that property is not as sacred as the laws of God, and that there is not a force of law and public justice to protect it, anarchy and tyranny commence. Property must be secured or liberty cannot exist."

John Adams[1]

FROM THE PROPHETS:

"Utopian and communitarian schemes which eliminate property rights are not only unworkable, they deny to man his inherent desire to improve his station. They are therefore contrary to the pursuit of happiness. With no property rights, man's incentive would be diminished to satisfying only his barest necessities such as food and clothing. How this truth is evident in the communist countries today! No property rights, no incentive to individual enterprise to risk one's own capital because the fruits of one's labor could not be enjoyed. No property rights, no contractual relationship to buy and sell because title to possession of goods could not be granted. No property rights, no recognition of divine law which prohibits man from stealing and coveting others' possessions; one cannot steal that which belongs to everyone, nor can he covet that which is not another's. No property rights, no possibility of the sanctity of one's own home and the joy which comes from creation, production and ownership... Charity, the greatest of godly virtues, would never be possible without property rights, for one cannot give what one does not own."

Ezra Taft Benson[2]

FROM THE SCRIPTURES:

"We believe that no government can exist in peace, except such laws are framed and held inviolate as will secure to each individual the free exercise of conscience, *the right and control of property*, and the

---

1 Philip B. Kurland and Ralph Lerner, Ed., *The Founders' Constitution,* (Chicago: University of Chicago Press) 6:8—9

2 Ezra T. Benson, *The Teachings of Ezra Taft Benson* (Bookcraft Pubs, 1988), 608.

protection of life. We believe that men should appeal to the civil law for redress of all wrongs and grievances, where personal abuse is inflicted or the *right of property* or character infringed, where such laws exist as will protect the same; but we believe that all men are justified in defending themselves, their friends, *and property*, and the government, from the unlawful assaults and encroachments of all persons in times of exigency, where immediate appeal cannot be made to the laws, and relief afforded."

Doctrine and Covenants 134:2, 11 *(emphasis added)*

STORY TO ILLUSTRATE THE PRINCIPLE:

William Bradford and the Pilgrims

From: Roland Usher, *The Story of the Pilgrims*
(Macmillan Co., 1937) 85-96, abridged.

Original grammar and spelling maintained.

The first years at Plymouth were years of starvation and hardship. Sickness claimed the lives of nearly half of the original passengers on the Mayflower their first winter. Before the next winter, a new shipload of settlers came, but they came without provisions of any kind. The pilgrims had to find ways to share their already meager supplies. By this time their clothes were worn to rags and their shoes were either full of holes or had gone to pieces entirely. They looked so ragged and forlorn that everyone who came pitied them.

The harvest of the second year was good but not good enough to feed as many extra mouths as they had guests during the year, and to keep themselves in plenty.

In the third year they were again in great want and saw that long before the new harvest, bread would be entirely gone. Governor Bradford summoned a council of important men and told them how serious the situation was.

"We came over here," he said, "in debt to the merchants who loaned us the money for our tools and expenses. We agreed to work and live in common for seven years so that we might pay that debt."

"What has been the result? The lazy do not work because they know that their food depends upon the common store and that we shall not be cruel enough to deprive them of their food because they do not work. The diligent, therefore, must work hard enough to provide for the lazy as well as for themselves. Besides, the women and children grumble at working in the fields, and the fathers have felt, quite naturally, that they did not wish their wives and children to work in order to support the slackers."

"The trouble," said Winslow, "lies with the system itself; with the common stock, the agreement to put all of what we raise and own into one store from which everyone shall be supplied and fed."

"I agree with you," said Bradford. "And I!" "And I!" came various voices around him.

"There is a solution," declared Bradford, "and only one. We must stop working the land together. Each man shall have as many acres as it seems possible he can plant and tend. He shall then have whatever he can raise on it for himself and his family and no one else shall be fed from it. The lazy will also be given fields and they will understand that if they do not work they will not eat."

"Yes," said Mr. Allerton, "I am sure that will please many. The women and children will then be able to work on their own fields. We shall not only find that those who are now lazy will work, when they are afraid that they will otherwise have no food, but we shall also get work from many people who now do not do any for other and better reasons."

So the land was divided, each family getting a large piece, and each single man getting as much as he could till. And they all worked very much harder than they ever had before and saw clearly that this was a good solution. The moment they devoted all of the attention to raising food they saw they would raise enough.

Adapting for Families:

Principle: We have more freedom when we own things and when government can't take those things away from us or tell us what to do with them.

Simple Explanation: The things a person owns are his to keep and to use like he wants to so he can accomplish whatever he would like to accomplish. If anyone tries to take those things away from him or to tell him what he can and can't do with them, then they are limiting his freedom. Government's job is to make sure these things don't happen, not to own things or to control what people own.

Discussion Questions:

1. How do you treat things that are yours differently than you treat things that are shared by everyone?
2. Do you like sharing everything or do you like having some things that are just your own?
3. How does personal ownership relate to our government and to governments throughout the world

See page 139 in the appendix for more references and quotes about Private Property.

Principle 10
FREEDOM OF RELIGION

Freedom is best preserved when men form government to respect people's liberty to worship according to the dictates of their own conscience.

EXPLANATION:

All civil societies operate on a moral code of right and wrong. Religion is important to society because it can provide this foundation, but only if it is believed in freely, not through compulsion. Those who are compelled by their government to accept or reject religious doctrines do so out of fear and compliance, rather than out of choice and devotion, which eventually erodes the moral foundations of that society.

FROM THE CONSTITUTION:

"Congress shall make no law respecting an establishment of religion, or prohibiting the free exercise thereof."

1st Amendment

FROM THE FOUNDING FATHERS:

"While we assert for ourselves a freedom to embrace, to profess, and to observe, the Religion which we believe to be of divine origin, we cannot deny an equal freedom to them whose minds have not yielded to the evidence which has convinced us."

James Madison[1]

---

1 Philip B. Kurland and Ralph Lerner, Ed., *The Founders' Constitution* (Chicago: University of Chicago Press) 8:298—304

FROM THE PROPHETS:

"Am I to disobey the law of God? Has any man a right to control my conscience, or your conscience, or to tell me I shall believe this or believe the other, or reject this or reject the other? No man has a right to do it. These principles are sacred, and the forefathers of this nation felt so and so proclaimed it in the Constitution of the United States, and said, 'Congress shall make no law respecting an establishment of religion, or prohibiting the free exercise thereof.'"

John Taylor[2]

FROM THE SCRIPTURES:

"We believe that religion is instituted of God; and that men are amenable to him, and to him only, for the exercise of it, unless their religious opinions prompt them to infringe upon the rights and liberties of others; but we do not believe that human law has a right to interfere in prescribing rules of worship to bind the consciences of men, nor to dictate forms for public or private devotion; that the civil magistrate should restrain crime, but never control conscience; should punish guilt, but never suppress the freedom of the soul. We believe that rulers, states, and governments have a right, and are bound to enact laws for the protection of all citizens in the free exercise of their religious belief; but we do not believe that they have a right in justice to deprive citizens of this privilege, or proscribe them in their opinions, so long as a regard and reverence are shown to the laws and such religious opinions do not justify sedition nor conspiracy. We do not believe it just to mingle religious influence with civil government, whereby one religious society is fostered and another proscribed in its spiritual privileges, and the individual rights of its members, as citizens, denied."

Doctrine and Covenants 134:4, 7, 9

---

2 Geo F. Gibbs and John Irvine, Ed., *Journal of Discourses by President John Taylor* (Liverpool: John Henry Smith), 152.

STORY TO ILLUSTRATE THE PRINCIPLE:

Charles V: The King Who Filled the World With Woe

From: Charles C. Coffin, *The Story of Liberty* (New York: Harper & Brothers, 1878), 293-297

Original grammar and spelling maintained.

Never before was there an assembly in Brussels like that which gathers in the great audience-chamber of the king's palace on October 25th, 1555. Princes, nobles, dukes, lords, ladies, archbishops, and a crowd of church prelates are there. The clock strikes three, and those for whom they are waiting enter the hall. Who are they? There comes a broad-shouldered man, with an ugly face, shaggy beard, white hair, crooked nose, and large underlip. He has lost all his teeth, except a few stubs. Once he was straight as an arrow; but now he walks with a crutch, and has to lean upon another's arm. He looks to be seventy, yet is only fifty-five. It is Charles, Emperor of Germany, King of Spain, Naples, and the Netherlands–the man before whom Doctor Martin Luther made his plea for liberty at Worms. For more than a third of a century Charles has been at war–his armies marching through Spain, Germany, France and Italy. He has an empire in the New World larger than all his domains in Europe, for, since he came to the throne, Hernando Cortez has overturned the thrones of Montezuma. They have discovered the Pacific Ocean, have found mountains of silver and gold in Peru. They have been in the Floridas, and marched under de Soto to the Mississippi. His empire is greater than that ruled by Caesar. Although he is so great a potentate, the gout has got hold of him. He is an enormous eater. At five o'clock in the morning he eats a chicken fricasseed in sweetened milk; then he has a long nap. At twelve o'clock he has a superb dinner of twenty dishes, and drinks a bottle of wine. At four o'clock he eats his first supper, a heartier meal than his dinner, with pastry and sweetmeats, and drinks goblets of beer. At midnight he eats his second supper, and drinks more beer. He is always hungry, yet everything tastes alike; for, abusing his stomach, he has lost the sense of taste.

The man upon whose arm he leans is only twenty-two, tall, handsome, with dark-brown hair, broad forehead, and clearly cut features. He has brown eyes, and wears a mustache and a beard. Although he is so young, he has been appointed commander-in-chief of the army which has been fighting against Admiral Coligny, general of the French armies. People call him William the Silent and Prince of Orange. Let us keep him in remembrance, for, of all the men that walk the earth, few will do more for liberty than he.

Behind the emperor comes Philip, with spindle-legs, a face like his father's, twenty-eight years old, proud, gross, eater of bacon-fat. Little regard has he for justice. What cares he for the rights and liberties of men? Nothing.

One of the bishops is Antony Perronot, of Arras, who can speak seven languages. He has been Charles's chief adviser. He detests the people, and hates heretics. The year after Charles was elected emperor he persuaded him to issue an edict against heretics. These were some of the provisions:

"No one shall print, write, copy, keep, conceal, sell, buy or give in the churches, streets, or other places, any book written by Martin Luther or any other heretic.

"Any person who teaches or reads the Bible, any person who says anything against the Church or its teachings, shall be executed.

"Any person who gives food or shelter to a heretic shall be burned to death. Any person who is *suspected,* although it may not appear that he has violated the command, after being once admonished, shall be put to death.

"If any one has knowledge of a heretic, and does not make it known to the court, he shall be put to death.

"An informer against a heretic shall recover one-half of the estates of the accused. If any one be present at a meeting of heretics, and shall inform against them, he shall have full pardon."

Torture-chambers are established. Thousands are put to death. The prisons are filled with accused heretics. Other thousands flee the country, seeking a refuge where no priest shall find them, or where they may be free from persecution. Their estates were confiscated, the property being divided between the men who ask questions, the king, and those who inform against the heretics.

Charles has wrenched money from the people of Holland to enable him to carry on his wars in Germany and Italy. He has trampled on their ancient rights and privileges, making him a despot. But he is weary of life, and is about to resign his crown to Philip. This is the day selected for his abdication. Since he came to the throne he has burned, or hanged, or otherwise put to death, more than one hundred thousand men and women for reading the Bible. He began to burn them in 1523. The first victims were two monks, who were burned in Brussels. The priests incited the people to hunt the heretics out of the land. Not a week passed, scarcely a day, that there was not a burning of heretics; but though so many were disposed of, they seemed to multiply faster than ever. In 1535, Charles issued another edict. Thus it ran:

"All heretics shall be put to death.

"If a man who has been a heretic recants, he may be killed by the sword, instead of being burned to death.

"If a woman who has been a heretic repents, she may be buried alive, instead of being burned."

For twenty years this has been the law of the land, and the smoke of the burning has been going up to heaven all the time.

Through all these years the emperor has been plundering the Netherlanders, wrenching from them more than two million dollars per annum. Through all these years he has been crushing out the liberties of the State and trampling upon the rights of the people. While heretics are burning, he gives thanks to God for permitting him to carry out such a glorious work. He is very religious–he will not eat meat on Friday, goes regularly to mass, counts his beads, says his prayers, and yet looks on with glee while men and women are smouldering in the flames.

The scene is over. Philip wears the crown, and Charles sails to Spain. He goes to Valladolid; and the bishops and priests of the Inquisition get up a jubilee in his honor–the burning of forty men, women and children, who have dared to think for themselves. So this man who has filled the world with woe–retires to spend the remainder of his life in seclusion, not fasting and praying, but eating like a glutton, reading despatches, counselling Philip–requiring him to hang and burn till there shall not be a heretic remaining in all his dominions. Even in his retirement he fills the world with woe.

ADAPTING FOR FAMILIES:

Principle: We have more freedom when government doesn't interfere with religion.

Simple Explanation: Heavenly Father wants us to worship how, where, and what we want to. He does not want us to be forced by government or anyone else. Remember that force was part of Satan's plan, and that we sided with Christ's plan so we could use our agency to choose how to worship.

DISCUSSION QUESTIONS:

1. Why does Heavenly Father allow us to worship Him instead of force us worship Him?
2. Why it so important for governments to allow people to worship as they please?

See page 109 in the appendix for more references and quotes about Freedom of Religion.

Principle 11
FREE MARKET

Freedom is best preserved when men form government to allow free market forces to control economic choices.

EXPLANATION:

True freedom, economic or otherwise, comes as individuals are able to make decisions and reap the consequences for their actions. The freedom to buy, sell, succeed, and fail are forces that no man or entity controls. The only role of government in a free market should be to secure rights, then the free market will reward or punish those who learn its laws and abide by its principles. When government is allowed to manipulate the forces of the free market, it places itself in the unnatural state of choosing winners and losers and of forcing market participants to act in ways that please government rather than in ways that satisfy the natural laws of supply and demand. When this occurs, the natural efficiency of the market is diminished or destroyed and the individual's freedom to do as he pleases is reduced.

FROM THE CONSTITUTION:

"No State shall . . . pass any . . . law impairing the obligation of contracts."

Article I, Section 10, Clause 1

FROM THE FOUNDING FATHERS:

"With all these blessings, what more is necessary to make us a happy and prosperous people? Still one thing more, fellow citizens - a wise and frugal government, which shall restrain men from injuring one another, shall leave them otherwise free to regulate their own pursuits of industry and improvement, and shall not take from the mouth of labor the bread it has earned. This is the sum of good government."

Thomas Jefferson[1]

1 Jefferson, Thomas. 1801. "First Inaugural Address" (speech). Text transcript from The Avalon Project at Yale Law School. http://avalon.law.yale.edu/19th_century/jefinau1.asp

FROM THE PROPHETS:

"Why, then, do Americans bake more bread, manufacture more shoes and assemble more TV sets than Russians do? They do so precisely because our government does not guarantee these things. If it did there would be so many accompanying taxes, controls, regulations and political manipulations that the productive genius that is America's would soon be reduced to the floundering level of waste and inefficiency now found behind the Iron Curtain. When government presumes to demand more and more of the fruits of a man's labor through taxation and reduces more and more his actual income by printing money and furthering debt, the wage earner is left with less and less to buy food, to provide housing, medical care, education and private welfare. The individuals are left without a choice and must look to the state as its benevolent supporter of these services. When that happens liberty is gone."

Ezra Taft Benson[2]

FROM THE SCRIPTURES:

"And it came to pass that the Lamanites did also go whithersoever they would, whether it were among the Lamanites or among the Nephites; and thus they did have free intercourse one with another, to buy and to sell, and to get gain, according to their desire. And it came to pass that they became exceedingly rich, both the Lamanites and the Nephites..."

Helaman 6:8-9

STORY TO ILLUSTRATE THE PRINCIPLE:

Sir Titus Salt

From: Sara K. Bolton, *Lives of Poor Boys Who Became Famous* (Thomas Y. Crowell Co., 1885) 123-129, abriged.

Original grammar and spelling maintained.

Titus Salt, a poor boy in England, was the son of a plain Yorkshire man. By the age of nineteen, he could be seen in a loose, dirty shirt, sorting and washing wool. At the age of thirty-three, happening

2 Benson, Ezra T. 1977. "Freedom and Free Enterprise" (speech). Text transcript from Latter-day Conservative. http://www.latterdayconservative.com/ezra-taft-benson/freedom-and-free-enterprise/

to be in Liverpool, he observed on the docks some huge pieces of dirty-looking alpaca wool. They had long lain in the warehouses, and, becoming a nuisance to the owners, were soon to be re-shipped to Peru. Young Salt took away a handful of the wool in his handkerchief, scoured and combed it, and was amazed at its attractive appearance. His father and friends advised him strongly to have nothing to do with the dirty stuff, as he could sell it to no one; and if he attempted to make cloth from it himself, he ran a great risk of failure. Finally he said, "I am going into this alpaca affair right and left, and I'll either make myself a man or a mouse."

Returning to Liverpool, he bought the whole three hundred bales for a small sum, and toiled diligently till proper machinery was made for the new material. The result was a great success. In three years over two million pounds of alpaca wool were imported. Employment was soon furnished to thousands, laborers coming from all over Great Britain and Germany. Ten years later Mr. Salt was made mayor; ten years after this a member of Parliament, and ten years later still a baronet by Queen Victoria, a great change from the poor boy in his soiled coarse shirt, but he deserved it all.

He was a remarkable man in many ways. Even when worth his millions, and giving lavishly on every hand, he would save blank leaves and scraps of paper for writing, and lay them aside for future use. He was an early riser, always at the works before the engines were started. It used to be said of him, "Titus Salt makes a thousand pounds before others are out of bed." He was punctual to the minute, most exact, and unostentatious. After he was knighted, it was no uncommon thing for him to take a poor woman and her baby in the carriage beside him, or a tired workman, or scatter hundreds of tracts in a village where he happened to be. Once a gypsy, not knowing who he was, asked him to buy a broom. To her astonishment, he bought all she was carrying!

The best of his acts, one which he had thought out carefully, as he said, "to do good to his fellowmen,' was the building of Saltaire for his four thousand workmen. When asked once what he had been reading of late, he replied, "Alpaca. If you had four or five thousand people to provide for every day, you would not have much time left for reading." Saltaire is a beautiful place on the banks of the river Aire, clean and restful. In the centre of the town stands the great six-story mill, well-ventilated, lighted, and warmed, five hundred and forty-five feet long, of light-colored stone.

The homes of the work people are an honor to the capitalist. They are of light stone, like the mill, two stories high, each containing parlor, kitchen, pantry, and three bedrooms or more, well ventilated and tasteful. Flowerbeds are in every front yard, with a vegetable garden in the rear. No broken carts or rubbish are to be seen. Mr. Salt provides school buildings, Italian in style–as are the other buildings–a hospital for sick or injured, and forty-five pretty little almshouses, like Italian villas, where the aged and infirm have a comfortable home. His workers are paid well.

Perhaps the most interesting of all Mr. Salt's gifts to his workmen is the Saltaire Club and Institute, a handsome building, with a large reading-room supplied with daily papers and current literature, a library, lecture-hall for eight hundred persons, a "School of Art," with models, drawings, and good teachers, a billiard-room with four tables, a room for scientific study, each student having proper appliances for laboratory work, a gymnasium and drill-room nearly sixty feet square, an armory for rifle practice and a smoking room, although Mr. Salt did not smoke.

Opposite the great mill is a dining-hall where a plate of meat can be purchased for four cents, a bowl of soup for two cents, and a cup of tea or coffee for one cent. If the men prefer to bring their own food, it is cooked free of charge. The manager had a fixed salary so that there is no temptation to scrimp the buyers.

Still another gift was made to the work people: a park of fourteen acres, with croquet and archery grounds, music pavilions, places for boating and swimming, and walks with beautiful flowers. Sir Titus Salt's last gift to his workmen was a Sunday-school building, where are held the "model Sunday schools of the country," say those who have attended the meetings.

No wonder, at the death of this man, 40,000 people came to his burial, members of Parliament, clergymen, workingmen's unions, and ragged schools. No wonder that statues have been erected to his memory, and that thousands go every year to Saltaire, to see what one capitalist has done for his laborers. No fear of strikes in his workshops; no socialism talked in the clean and pretty homes of the men; no squalid poverty; no depraving ignorance.

That capital is feeling its responsibility in this matter of homes for laborers is one of the hopeful signs of the times. We shall come, sometime, to believe with the late President Chadbourne, "The rule now commonly acted upon is that business must be cared for, and men must care for themselves. The principles of action, in the end, must be that men must be cared for, and business must be subservient to this great work."

If, as Spurgeon has well said, "Home is the grandest of all institutions," capital can do no better work than look to the homes of the laborer. It is not the mansion which the employer builds for himself, but the house which he builds for his employee, which will insure a safe country for his children to dwell in. If discontent and poverty surround the palace, its foundations are weak; if intelligence has been disseminated, and comfort promoted by his unselfish thought for others, then he leaves a goodly heritage for his children.

ADAPTING FOR FAMILIES:

Principle: We have more freedom when government doesn't interfere with businesses like stores, manufacturing companies, or banks.

Simple Explanation: It is very important for people to buy and sell things so they can live. It should be up to each person and not to the government to decide what to spend their money on, what to make, what to sell, and at what price. That way whether a person succeeds or fails won't be based on government but it will be based on their own choices. It is important for government to make sure that people are honest with each other so that people can buy and sell fairly with each other.

DISCUSSION QUESTIONS:

1. Why is it important that you get to choose how you spend your time and your money?

2. What is the difference between government choosing winners and losers and the free market choosing them?

See page 101 in the appendix for more references and quotes regarding the Free Market.

Principle 12
AVOID DEBT

Freedom is best preserved when men form government to avoid the bondage of debt.

EXPLANATION:

An individual or nation that is in debt is in bondage to their creditor. Once in debt, there are certain legal limits that separate the debtor in some degree from his life, liberty, and property, which limits his ability to act for himself. Debt is based on acquiring something that it is not yet fully paid for. Entering into debt is sometimes appropriate, but national debt too often represents unconstitutional government spending to provide for the wants of the undisciplined people it represents. Such a people subscribe to the false doctrine of getting "something for nothing" and are continually enslaved by their insatiable appetite for more, while giving little thought to the associated costs.

FROM THE CONSTITUTION:

"All debts contracted and Engagements entered into, before the Adoption of this Constitution, shall be as valid against the United States under this Constitution, as under the Confederation."

Article VI, Clause 1

(Too often, newly formed governments wrote off all debts acquired by the previous government, but the virtue of the Founding Fathers would not permit this.)

FROM THE FOUNDING FATHERS:

"I sincerely believe . . . that the principle of spending money to be paid by posterity, under the name of funding, is but swindling futurity on a large scale."

Thomas Jefferson[1]

---

1 Albert Allery Bergh, Ed., *The Writing of Thomas Jefferson* (New York: G.P. Putnam's Sons, 1892) 99.

From the Prophets:

"Self-reliance cannot obtain when there is serious debt hanging over a household. One has neither independence nor freedom from bondage when he is obligated to others."

Gordon B. Hinckley[2]

From the Scriptures:

"Pay the debt thou hast contracted with the printer. Release thyself from bondage."

Doctrine and Covenants 19:35

Story to Illustrate the Principle:

Robert Morris and the Risk of Debt

From: James Baldwin, *An American Book of Golden Deeds* (New York: American Book Company, 1907) 189-194, abridged.

Original grammar and spelling maintained.

When the united American colonies entered upon a long and precarious war with the mother country, they had as yet no efficient army; they had no money; but they felt a supreme faith in the righteousness of their cause.

Upon George Washington of Virginia devolved the task of organizing, equipping, and conducting the army. Upon Robert Morris of Pennsylvania devolved the task of supplying the funds for the carrying on of the war. Without the patriotic labors of both these men, it is not unreasonable to believe that the colonies would have failed to achieve their liberty and the war would have ended in disaster.

Robert Morris was at the head of the largest commercial house in Philadelphia; he was the leading man of business in America. In the Congress of 1775 he was active in pushing forward and sustaining the war, and people soon perceived that the country must very largely depend upon him for financial aid.

---

2 Hinckely, Gordon B. Oct. 1998. "*To the Boys and to the Men*" (speech). Text transcript from LDS.org. https://www.lds.org/general-conference/1998/10/to-the-boys-and-to-the-men?lang=eng

When the Declaration of Independence was proposed, Robert Morris voted against it. He was in favor of independence, but he did not believe the time was ripe for it. When the day came for adopting the Declaration, however, he signed it, and thus pledged his life and his fortune to the cause of liberty.

The months that followed were months of trial and great perplexity. How should the money be obtained for feeding and clothing and arming the patriot forces under Washington? It required all the skill and experience of Robert Morris to provide for the necessities of the new government. It required, also, an amount of self-sacrifice which few other men would have been willing to make.

Often he was obliged to borrow large sums of money, for which he became personally responsible. Through his exertions, three million rations of provisions were forwarded to the army just at the moment when such aid was most needed.

In the following year he was appointed superintendent of finance, or, as we should now say, secretary of the treasury, for the United States. But the treasury was empty; the Congress was in debt two and a half million dollars; the army was destitute; there was no one who would lend to the government; without some immediate aid the war could not go on. Nevertheless, people had confidence in Robert Morris, and it was that confidence which saved the day.

He began by furnishing the army with several thousand barrels of flour, pledging his own means to pay for it.

When Washington decided to make a bold campaign in Virginia against Lord Cornwallis, it was to Robert Morris that he looked for support.

"We are in want of food, of clothing, of arms," said the general. "We have not even the means of transporting the army from place to place or subsisting in the field."

"I myself," said Robert Morris, "will see that you are provided."

He hastened to borrow of his friends all the money they were willing to spare for the cause of liberty. He pledged his own means to the last shilling. He directed the commissary to send forward all necessary supplies for the army in Virginia. He procured boats for transporting troops and provisions. He left nothing undone; he spared no pains to make the campaign in Virginia a successful one. Washington's victory at Yorktown was to a large degree the result no less of his own skill and courage than of the energy and self-sacrifice of Robert Morris.

At the close of the war there was no money to pay off the soldiers and there was great dissatisfaction on every side. Robert Morris came forward, and by endorsing certificates in the amount of three quarters of a million dollars, relieved the public distress and made it possible to disband the army. While doing this, he again pledged himself personally to see that all the obligations that he had made in behalf of the government were properly satisfied.

It is pleasant to remember that the money which he had so generously advanced in aid of the cause of liberty was finally paid back to him, and that his faith in the honesty of the government was not misplaced.

And yet, this financier of the American Revolution, this patriot, statesman, merchant and man of personal and business integrity, passed the last years of his life in prison,–a prisoner for debt,–and was only saved from dying there by the kindly offices of a friend who unearthed an old claim in which Morris had an interest, and by making it yield a small income for the old patriot's wife, enabled him to die at home, free but poor, on the eighth of May, 1806.

It must be confessed that the disasters of Robert Morris came because of his own actions. But even of these we may say that he had so firm a belief in the future of the great Republic he had helped to found that he took "too much stock" in its immediate development. He went into speculations in land and building lots that proved too slow to meet his expectations, and saddled him so heavily with losses and obligations that all his property was swept away, and he failed for three millions of dollars–an enormous sum in those days of small things.

"You are over sixty, Morris," said Washington to him one day, in warning. "Don't go into these speculations, they will ruin you."

"I cannot help it, general," replied the old Financier. "I must go deep or not at all."

When the crash came he gave up everything to meet the demand upon him; but it could not save him from a debtor's prison. So to prison he went, an old and broken man; "but," as he wrote to his friend Alexander Hamilton, "I am sensible that I have lost the confidence of the world as to my pecuniary ability, but I believe not as to my honor or integrity."

Washington's friendship remained steadfast. He visited his old friend in prison, looked after his wife, and assured her of "the affectionate regard of General and Mrs. Washington for Robert Morris."

The best of men make mistakes, and it is not for us to attempt to excuse the extravagances and speculations of this old and tried business man. These now, however, should be forgotten and, rather than censure or criticism, the affectionate remembrance of this great and prosperous Republic should be for the man who made its greatness and prosperity possible, and in its days of storm and stress stood behind it with his credit and his name.

ADAPTING FOR FAMILIES:

Principle: We are most free when we don't owe money to others

Simple Explanation: When you owe money to others part of your freedom is taken away because you have to pay them back how and when they want you to. We should never enter into debt just so we can get things we really don't need. If we do, we are giving up our freedom for things that really aren't important.

DISCUSSION QUESTIONS:

1. What effect does debt have on our family? What are our plans to get out of debt?
2. What might happen to my freedom if I buy things I can't afford and don't really need?

See page 87 in the appendix for more references and quotes about Avoiding Debt

Appendix

Principles appear in alphabetical order

ACTIVELY ENGAGED

FROM THE CONSTITUTION:

"A well regulated Militia, being necessary to the security of a free State, the *right of the people* to keep and bear Arms, shall not be infringed." *(People must themselves be actively engaged in defending freedom).*

Amendment II *(emphasis added)*

"[The Congress shall have Power] to provide for calling forth the Militia to execute the Laws of the Union, suppress Insurrections and repel Invasions. To provide for organizing, arming, and disciplining, the Militia, and for governing such Part of them as may be employed in the Service of the United States, reserving to the States respectively, the Appointment of the Officers, and the Authority of training the Militia according to the discipline prescribed by Congress."

Article I, Section 8, Clauses 15-16

FROM THE FOUNDING FATHERS:

"Those who expect to reap the blessings of freedom must, like men, undergo the fatigues of supporting it."

Thomas Paine

Phillip S. Foner, *The Complete Writings of Thomas Paine, Vol.2* (New York: Citadel Press, 1945) 102.

"Knowledge will forever govern ignorance: And a people who mean to be their own Governors, must arm themselves with the power which knowledge gives."

James Madison

Philip B. Kurland and Ralph Lerner, Ed., *The Founders' Constitution*, (Chicago: University of Chicago Press), 9:103—9

FROM THE PROPHETS:

"Next to being one in worshiping God there is nothing in this world upon which this Church should be more united than in upholding and defending the Constitution of the United States! May the appeal of our Lord in His intercessory prayer for unity be realized in our homes, our wards, and stakes, and in our support of the basic principles of our Republic."

David O. Mckay

Andrew S. Weeks, *America in perspective: LDS perspectives on America's past, present and future* (San Jose: Writers Club Press, 2000), 57.

"Now Satan is anxious to neutralize the inspired counsel of the Prophet and hence keep the priesthood off-balance, ineffective and inert in the fight for freedom. He does this through diverse means including the use of perverse reasoning.

"For example, he will argue, 'There is no need to get involved in the fight for freedom – all you need to do is live the gospel.' Of course this is a contradiction, because we cannot fully live the gospel and not be involved in the fight for freedom.

"We would not say to someone, 'There is no need to be baptized – all you need to do is live the gospel.' That would be ridiculous because baptism is a part of the gospel.

"How would you have reacted if during the War in Heaven someone had said to you, 'Look, just do what's right, there is no need to get involved in the fight for free agency.' Now it is obvious what the devil is trying to do, but it is sad to see many of us fall for his destructive line.

"The cause of freedom is the most basic part of our religion.

"Our position on freedom helped get us to this earth, and it can make the difference as to whether we get back home or not."

Ezra Taft Benson

Ezra Taft Benson, *An Enemy Hath Done This* (Salt Lake City: Parliament Publishers, 1969), 314.

"For years we have heard of the role the elders could play in saving the Constitution from total destruction. But how can the elders be expected to save it if they have not studied it and are not sure if it is being destroyed or what is destroying it."

Ezra Taft Benson

Ezra Taft Benson. 1966. "Our Immediate Responsibility" (lecture, Brigham Young University, Provo, UT, Oct. 25, 1966).
https://speeches.byu.edu/talks/ezra-taft-benson_immediate-responsibility/

"We advocate the necessity of all members of the Church showing appreciation of your franchise, your citizenship, by voting, exercising your right to say who shall be your leaders. They become our servants. That is the spirit of the Constitution."

David O. McKay

David O. McKay, *Conference Report* (SLC: The Church of Jesus Christ of Latter-day Saints) October 1952, 128-131.

"The only way we can keep our freedom is to work at it. Not some of us. All of us. Not some of the time, but all of the time. So if you value your citizenship and you want to keep it for yourself and your children and their children, give it your faith, your belief, and give it your active support in civic affairs."

Spencer W. Kimball

Edward L. Kimball, *The Teachings of Spencer W. Kimball* (SLC: Deseret Book, 2006) 405.

"Unlike the political opportunist, the true statesman values principles above popularity and works to create popularity for those political principles which are wise and just."

Ezra Taft Benson

Ezra Taft Benson, *Conference Report October 1968*, (SLC: The Church of Jesus Christ of Latter-day Saints) 17

"It is good strategy to stand up for the right, even when it is unpopular. Perhaps I should say, especially when it is unpopular."

Ezra Taft Benson

Ezra Taft Benson, "Confidence in the Lord," *New Era* (August 1989), 36.

AVOID DEBT

FROM THE CONSTITUTION:

"The Congress shall have Power] To *coin money*, regulate the value thereof, and of foreign coin, and fix the standard of weights and measures." *(Not a power to print money. Coined money cannot be produced out of thin air.)*

Article I, Section 8, Clause 5 (*emphasis added)*

"The Congress shall have Power] To borrow money on the credit of the United States" *(Notice, not to "print" money, nor to borrow "paper" money, but to "borrow money").*

Article I, Section 8, Clause 2

FROM THE FOUNDING FATHERS:

"To compel a man to furnish contributions of money for the propagation of opinions which he disbelieves and abhors, is sinful and tyrannical."

Thomas Jefferson

Merril D. Peterson & Robert C. Vaughan, Ed., *The Virginia Statute for Religious Freedom: Its evolution and Consequences in American History* (England: Cambridge University Press, 1988).

"And to preserve their independence, we must not let our rulers load us with perpetual debt. We must make our election between *economy and liberty,* or *profusion and servitude."*

Thomas Jefferson

Thomas Jefferson, Paul Licester Ford, Ed., *The Works of Thomas Jefferson, vol. 12* (New York: G.*P.* Putnam's Sons, 1905), 10.

"It is incumbent on every generation to pay its own debts as it goes. A principle which, if acted on, would save one half the wars of the world."

Thomas Jefferson

Thomas Jefferson, *The Thomas Jefferson Papers at the Library of Congress* "Thomas Jefferson to Antoine Louis Claude Destutt de Tracy," (December 26, 1820). http://hdl.loc.gov/loc.mss/mtj.mtjbib023950

FROM THE PROPHETS:

"From my earliest recollections, from the days of Brigham Young until now, I have listened to men standing in the pulpit … urging the people not to run into debt; and I believe that the great majority of all our troubles today is caused through the failure to carry out that counsel."

Heber J. Grant

Heber J. Grant, *Conference Report Oct. 1921* (SLC: The Church of Jesus Christ of Latter-day Saints), 3.

"Do not leave yourself or your family unprotected against financial storms. … Build up savings."

Ezra Taft Benson

Ezra Taft Benson *Pay Thy Debt, and Live,* Brigham Young University Speeches of the Year (28 Feb. 1962), 10.

"Not only should we teach men to get out of debt but we should teach them likewise to stay out of debt."

Harold B. Lee

Clyde J. Williams, Ed., *The Teachings of Harold B. Lee* (1996), 315.

"Many of our people are living on the very edge of their incomes. In fact, some are living on borrowings. … I urge you to be modest in your expenditures; discipline yourselves in your purchases to avoid debt to the extent possible. Pay off debt as quickly as you can, and free yourselves from bondage."

Gordon B. Hinckley

Gordon B. Hinckley, "To the Boys and to the Men," *Liahona* (Jan. 1999) 65-66

"Many more people could ride out the storm-tossed waves in their economic lives if they had their year's supply of food … and were debt-free. Today we find that many have followed this counsel in reverse: they have at least a year's supply of debt and are food-free."

Thomas S. Monson

Thomas S. Monson "That Noble Gift—Love at Home," *Church News (*May 2001) 7.

FROM THE SCRIPTURES:

"The wicked borroweth, and payeth not again."

Psalms 37:21

"The borrower is servant to the lender."

Proverbs 22:7

"I forgave thee all that debt . . . Shouldest not thou also have had compassion?"

Matthew 18:32-33

"Owe no man any thing, but to love one another."

Romans 13:8

"Ye are eternally indebted to your Heavenly Father."

Mosiah 2:34

"Whosoever among you borroweth of his neighbor should return the thing that he borroweth."

Mosiah 4:28

"It is . . . forbidden, to get in debt to thine enemies."

Doctrine and Covenants 64:27

"Pay all your debts."

Doctrine and Covenants 104:78

"Let not my servant . . . get in debt any more for the building of a house unto my name."

Doctrine and Covenants 115:13

CHECKS AND BALANCES

FROM THE CONSTITUTION:

"If [the president] approve he shall sign it, but if not he shall return it, with is Objections to that House in which it shall have originated ... If after such Reconsideration two thirds of that House shall agree to pass the bill . . . and if approved by two thirds of [the other] House, it shall become a Law."*

Article I, Section 7, Clause 2

"In all other the other Cases before mentioned, the supreme Court shall have appellate Jurisdiction, both as to Law and Fact with such Exceptions, and under such Regulations as the Congress shall make." (Congress can decide which cases the Supreme Court can hear because we are a nation of we, the people, not of they, the 9 supreme court justices.)*

Article III, Section 2, Clause 2

"And [The President] shall nominate, and by and with the Advice and Consent of the Senate, shall appoint ... Judges of the supreme Court"*

Article II, Section 2, Clause 2

*Author's Note: *Notice that in all three cases, the Congress has the final say because the Congress is chosen by, representative of and accountable to we, the people, who are the source of all political power and authority by virtue of our God given rights.*

Legislative: "The Laws of Nature and of Nature's God", "All men are created equal, that they are endowed by their Creator with certain unalienable Rights" *(God is the great Lawgiver of the Universe)*

Executive: "With a firm reliance on the protection of divine Providence." *(God is the great Protector and Executor of the Universe)*

Judicial: "Appealing to the Supreme Judge of the world." *(God is the great Judge of the Universe)*

Declaration of Independence

FROM THE FOUNDING FATHERS:

"It will not be denied that power is of an encroaching nature and that it ought to be effectually restrained from passing the limits assigned to it."

James Madison

James Madison, *The Federalist Papers #48* (New York: Cosimo Classics, 2006) 321.

"What has destroyed liberty and the rights of man in every government which has ever existed under the sun? The generalizing and concentrating all cares and power into one body."

Thomas Jefferson

Thomas Jefferson, *The Founders' Constitution* (Chicago: The University of Chicago Press), 14: 421—23.

" A mere demarcation on parchment of the constitutional limits of the several departments, is not a sufficient guard against those encroachments which lead to a tyrannical concentration of all the powers of government in the same hands."

James Madison

James Madison, *The Federalist Papers #48* (New York : Cosimo Classics, 2006), 321.

"But the great security against a gradual concentration of the several powers in the same department, consists in giving to those who administer each department the necessary constitutional means and personal motives to resist encroachments of the others. The provision for defense must in this, as in all other cases, be made commensurate to the danger of attack. Ambition must be made to counteract ambition. The interest of the man must be connected with the constitutional rights of the place. It may be a reflection on human nature, that such devices should be necessary to control the abuses of government, But what is government itself, but the greatest of all reflections on human nature? If men were angels, no government would be necessary. If angels were to govern men, neither external nor internal controls on government would be necessary. In framing a government which is to be administered by men over men, the great difficulty lies in this: you must first enable the government to control the governed; and in the next place oblige it to control itself. A dependence on the people is, no doubt, the primary control on the government; but experience has taught mankind the necessity of auxiliary precautions."

James Madison

James Madison, *The Federalist Papers #51* (New York : Cosimo Classics, 2006), 337.

"The accumulation of all powers, legislative, executive, and judiciary, in the same hands, whether of one, a few, or many . . . may justly be pronounced the very definition of tyranny. . . . the preservation of liberty requires that the three great departments of power should be separate and distinct." James Madison

James Madison, *The Federalist Papers #47* (New York : Cosimo Classics, 2006), 313

FROM THE PROPHETS:

"The people should with jealous care guard against the time ever coming when any one of these three branches may surrender its rights to any other, or be swallowed up and overcome by some other branch of the government. Today there are many who advocate the destruction of these safeguards given us by the framers of the Constitution who were men inspired to make this document as near to the fundamental doctrines of the kingdom of God as it was possible under the circumstances for it to be."

Joseph Fielding Smith

Joseph Fielding Smith, *Conference Report April 1950* (SLC: The Church of Jesus Christ of Latter-day Saints), 153-159.

FROM THE SCRIPTURES:

Author's Note: *The three great powers, that each individual possesses, are the power to plan, the power to do, and the power to review. In our personal lives these powers are ours to employ as we live on this earth and as we progress through this mortal experience. In governmental terms, these same three powers are referred to as the power to legislate, the power to execute and the power to judge. In our Constitution, these three powers are rightfully separated into three branches in order to prevent their abuse on mans' freedom. As the Supreme Creator, Executor, and Judge of the world, (see Declaration of Independence reference below) God possesses and uses these three powers (personally and governmentally) as is evidenced in many scriptural references but particularly in the creation of the world as is taught in the 2nd chapter of Moses:*

"And I, God, said unto mine Only Begotten, which was with me from the beginning: Let us make man in our image, after our likeness *(the power to plan, to legislate)* ... And I, God, created man in mine own image, in the image of mine Only Begotten created I him *(the power to do, to execute)* … And I, God, saw everything that I had made, and, behold, all things which I had made were very good *(the power to review, to judge)*

Moses 2:26-27, 31

"Behold, it is not expedient that we should have a king; for thus saith the Lord: Ye shall not esteem one flesh above another, or one man shall not think himself above another; therefore I say unto you it is not expedient that ye should have a king… I desire that ye should stand fast in this liberty wherewith ye have been made free, and that ye trust no man to be a king over you."

Mosiah 23:7, 13

"Let us appoint judges, to judge this people according to our law; and we will newly arrange the affairs of this people, for we will appoint wise men to be judges, that will judge this people according to the commandments of God."

Mosiah 29:11

"Judgment goeth before the face of him who sitteth upon the throne and governeth and executeth all things." *(God is the governor, executor and judge)*

Doctrine and Covenants 88:40

FEDERALISM

FROM THE CONSTITUTION:

"We, the people . . ."

Preamble to the Constitution

"Each House shall keep a Journal of its Proceedings, and from time to time publish the same . . ." *(open, transparent to the people.)*

Article I, Sec. 5, Clause 3

"The enumeration in the Constitution, of certain rights, shall not be construed to deny or disparage others retained by the people."

9th Amendment

"The House of Representatives shall be composed of Members chosen every second Year by the People of the several States"*

Article I, Section 2, Clause 1

"The Senate of the United States shall be composed of two Senators from each state chosen by the legislature thereof for six years."*

Article I, Section 3, Clause 1

*Author's note: *Previous to the 17th amendment, people were represented at the federal level in the House and the States were represented at the federal level in the Senate (i.e. federalism - different levels of government, each represented)*

"No State shall, without the consent of Congress ..."**

Article I, Section 10, Clauses 1-3

**Author's Note: *The Constitution identifies powers States cannot use and others they can only use when authorized by Congress. (i.e. federalism - different levels of government have different responsibilities)*

FROM THE FOUNDING FATHERS:

"The people of these United States are the rightful masters of both congresses and courts, not to overthrow the Constitution, but to overthrow the men who pervert the Constitution."

Abraham Lincoln *(not a founding father, but a good quote)*

Abraham Lincoln, *Political Debates Between Lincoln and Douglas* (Cleveland: Burrows Bros. Co., 1897).

"Whenever a question arises between the society at large and any magistrate vested with powers originally delegated by that society, it must be decided by the voice of the society itself: there is not upon earth any other tribunal to resort to."

William Blackstone *(not a founding father, but a good quote)*

Sir William Blackstone, *Commentaries on the Laws of England* (Philadelphia : J.B. Lippincott & Co., 1859) 160.

"In the compound republic of America, the power surrendered by the people is first divided between two distinct governments, and then the portion allotted to each subdivided among distinct and separate departments. Hence a double security arises to the rights of the people. The different governments will control each other, at the same time that each will be controlled by itself."

James Madison

James Madison, *The Federalist Papers #51* (New York : Cosimo Classics, 2006), 339

"In the former case [national governments], all local authorities are subordinate to the supreme; and may be controlled, directed, or abolished by it at pleasure. In the latter, the local or municipal authorities form distinct and independent portions of the supremacy, no more subject, within their respective spheres, to the general authority, than the general authority is subject to them, within its own sphere. In this relation, then, the proposed government cannot be deemed a *national* one; since its jurisdiction extends to certain enumerated objects only, and leaves to the several States a residuary and inviolable sovereignty over all other objects.

James Madison

James Madison, *The Federalist Papers #39* (New York : Cosimo Classics, 2006), 248-249.

"The powers delegated by the proposed Constitution to the federal government, are few and defined. Those which are to remain in the State governments are numerous and indefinite. The former will be exercised principally on external objects, as war, peace, negotiation, and foreign commerce; with which last the power of taxation will, for the most part, be connected. The powers reserved to the several States will extend to all the objects which, in the ordinary course of affairs, concern the lives, liberties, and properties of the people, and the internal order, improvement, and prosperity of the State."

James Madison

James Madison and Alexander Hamilton, *The Federalist Papers #45* (New York : Cosimo Classics, 2006), 303

"But ambitious encroachments of the federal government, on the authority of the State governments, would not excite the opposition of a single State, or of a few States only. They would be signals of general alarm."

James Madison

James Madison, *The Federalist Papers #48* (New York : Cosimo Classics, 2006), 309.

From the Prophets:

"Many persons suppose that there is some provision in the United States Constitution touching this subject. This is an error. The Constitution leaves all matters relating to marriage to be regulated by the people of the various States; and hence it is that so many diversified marriage and divorce codes exist throughout the country."

John Taylor

O. Everett, *North American Review, Vol. 326* (Boston, 1884) 5.

"We stand proudly erect in the consciousness of our rights as American citizens, and plant ourselves firmly on the sacred guarantees of the Constitution; and that instrument, while it defines the powers and privileges of the President, Congress and the judiciary, also directly provides that 'the powers not delegated to the United States by the Constitution, nor prohibited by it to the States, are reserved to the States, respectively or to the people.'"

John Taylor

John Henry Smith, *Journal of Discourses, Vol. 23* (Liverpool, 1883) 67.

From the Scriptures:

"And it came to pass that the people desired of them that they should anoint one of their sons to be a king over them. And now behold, this was grievous unto them. And the brother of Jared said unto hem: Surely this thing leadeth into captivity."

Ether 6:22-23

"[The king-men] were desirous that the law should be altered in a manner to overthrow the free government and to establish a king over the land. … And it came to pass that Moroni commanded that his army should go against those king-men, to pull down their pride and their nobility and level them with the earth, or they should take up arms and support the cause of liberty."

Alma 51:5, 17

"Behold, it is not expedient that we should have a king; for thus saith the Lord: Ye shall not esteem one flesh above another, or one man shall not think himself above another; therefore I say unto you it is not expedient that ye should have a king… I desire that ye should stand fast in this liberty wherewith ye have been made free, and that ye trust no man to be a king over you."

Mosiah 23:7, 13

"And I command you to do these things in the fear of the Lord; and I command you to do these things, and that ye have no king; that if these people commit sins and iniquities they shall be answered upon their own heads. For behold I say unto you, the sins of many people have been caused by the iniquities of their kings; therefore their iniquities are answered upon the heads of their kings. And now I desire that this inequality should be no more in this land, especially among this my people; but I desire that this land be a land of liberty, and every man may enjoy his rights and privileges alike … that the burden should come upon all the people, that every man might bear his part. … And now it came to pass, … [that] they were convinced of the truth of his words. Therefore they relinquished their desires for a king, and became exceedingly anxious that every man should have an equal chance throughout all the land; yea, and every man expressed a willingness to answer for his own sins."

Mosiah 29:30-38

Free Market

From the Constitution:

"[The Congress shall have Power] to coin Money, regulate the Value thereof."

Article I, Section 8, Clause 5

"No Tax or Duty shall be laid on Articles exported from any State. No Preference shall be given by any Regulation of Commerce or Revenue to the Ports of one State over those of another; nor shall Vessels bound to, or from, one State, be obliged to enter, clear, or pay Duties in another." (the Federal government shouldn't be setting different tax rates for different states nor should it allow states to place arbitrary fees on each other).

Article I, Section 9, Clauses 5-6

"[The Congress shall have Power] To provide for the Punishment of counterfeiting the Securities and current Coin of the United States."

Article I, Section 8, Clause 6

From the Founding Fathers:

"Socialism, like the ancient ideas from which it springs, confuses the distinction between government and society. As a result of this, every time we object to a thing being done by government, the socialists conclude that we object to its being done at all. We disapprove of state education. Then the socialists say that we are opposed to any education. We object to a state religion. Then the socialists say that we want no religion at all. We object to a state-enforced equality. Then they say that we are against equality. And so on, and so on. It is as if the socialists were to accuse us of not wanting persons to eat because we do not want the state to raise grain."

Frédéric Bastiat *(not a founding father, but a great quote)*

Frédéric Bastiat, *The Law* (New York: Cosimo Classics, 2006) 26

"Let vigorous methods be adopted; not to limit the prices of articles, for this I believe is inconsistent with the very nature of things, and impracticable in itself, but to … promote … private economy; encourage manufacturers, etc."

George Washington

Dave Gaffney, *These Things Must Happen* (OK: Tate Publishing and Enterprises, 2011) 170.

"The utopian schemes of levelling, and a community of goods, are as visionary and impracticable, as those which vest all property in the Crown, are arbitrary, despotic, and, in our government unconstitutional."

Samuel Adams

Harry Alonzo Cushing, Ed., *The Writings of Samuel Adams, Vol. 1* (New York: G.P. Putnam's Sons, 1904) 137.

"If we can prevent the government from wasting the labors of the people under the pretense of taking care of them, they must become happy."

Thomas Jefferson

Andrew A. Lipscomb and Albert Ellery Bergh, Ed., *The Writings of Thomas Jefferson* (Washington: Thomas Jefferson Memorial Association, 1905) 342.

"The Americans make associations to give entertainments, to found seminaries, to build inns, to construct churches, to diffuse books, to send missionaries to the antipodes; in this manner they found hospitals, prisons, and schools. If it is proposed to inculcate some truth or to foster some feeling by the encouragement of a great example, they form a society. Wherever at the head of some new undertaking you see the government in France, or a man of rank in England, in the United States you will be sure to find an association. … I have often admired the extreme skill with which the inhabitants of the United States succeed in proposing a common object for the exertions of a great many men and in inducing them voluntarily to pursue it"

Alexis de Toqueville *(not a founding father, but a great quote)*

Alexis de Toqueville, *Democracy in America* (New York, 2003) 512-513.

"But let them [members of the parliament of Great Britain] not think to exclude us from going to other markets, to dispose of those commodities which they cannot use, nor to supply those wants which they cannot supply. Still less let it be proposed that our properties within our own territories shall be taxed or regulated by any power on earth but our own. The god who gave us life gave us liberty at the same time: the hand of force may destroy, but cannot disjoin them."

Thomas Jefferson

Boyd, Julian P., Charles T. Cullen, John Catanzariti, Barbara B. Oberg, Eds., *The Papers of Thomas Jefferson, Vol. 1* (Princeton: Princeton University Press, 1950) 135.

From the Prophets:

"Governments are the *servants*, not the *masters* of the people. All who love the Constitution of the United States can vow with Thomas Jefferson, who, when he was president, said,

'I have sworn upon the altar of God eternal hostility against every form of tyranny over the mind of man.'

He later said:

'To preserve our independence, we must not let our rulers load us with perpetual debt. We must take our choice between economy and liberty, or profusion and servitude. If we run into such debts, we must be taxed in our meat and drink, in our necessities and in our comforts, in our labors and in our amusements.

'If we can prevent the government from wasting the labors of the people under pretense of caring for them, they will be happy. The same prudence which in private life would forbid our paying our money for unexplained projects, forbids it in the disposition of public money. We are endeavoring to reduce the government to the practice of rigid economy to avoid burdening the people and arming the magistrate with a patronage of money which might be used to corrupt the principles of our government.'

. . .In conclusion, I repeat that no greater immediate responsibility rests upon members of the Church, upon all citizens of this Republic and of neighboring Republics than to protect the freedom vouchsafed by the Constitution of the United States.

Let us, by exercising our privileges under the Constitution—

(1) Preserve our right to worship God according to the dictates of our conscience,

(2) Preserve the right to work when and where we choose. No free man should be compelled to pay tribute in order to realize this God-given privilege. Read in the Doctrine and Covenants this statement:

. . . it is not right that any man should be in bondage one to another (D&C 101:79).

(3) Feel free to plan and to reap without the handicap of bureaucratic interference.

(4) Devote our time, means, and life if necessary, to hold inviolate those laws which will secure to each individual the free exercise of conscience, the right and control of property, and the protection of life.

To sum up this whole question: In these days of uncertainty and unrest, liberty-loving people's greatest responsibility and paramount duty is to preserve and proclaim the freedom of the individual, his relationship to Deity, and, (repeating the message of our President, to which I subscribe with all my soul) the necessity of obedience to the principles of the gospel of Jesus Christ—only thus will mankind find peace and happiness ..."

David O. McKay

David O. McKay, *Conference Report April 1950* (SLC: The Church of Jesus Christ of Latter-day Saints), 31-37.

"The Constitution expressly says that no law shall be passed impairing the obligation of contracts. But we have entered into covenants and contracts in our most sacred places ...and yet the attempt is now being made to give ... law an *ex post facto* application and to punish us for these contracts which were not criminal ... at the time they were formed. ... I have never broken any law of these United States. . . ."

John Taylor

John Henry Smith, *Journal of Discourses* (Liverpool, 1884) 153.

"I consider that it is not only prudential, but absolutely necessary to protect the inhabitants of this city from being imposed upon by a spurious currency ... I think it much safer to go upon the hard money system altogether. I have examined the Constitution upon this subject and find my doubts removed"

Joseph Smith

Charles W. Penrose, Ed., *The Latter-day Saints' Millennial Star, Vol. 20* (London: Calkin, 1858) 616.

"Communism being thus hostile to loyal American citizenship and incompatible with true Church membership, of necessity no loyal American citizen and no faithful Church member can be a Communist. We call upon all Church members completely to eschew Communism. The safety of our divinely inspired Constitutional government and the welfare of our Church imperatively demand that Communism shall have no place in America."

Heber J. Grant

Grant, Heber J., 1977. "A Vision and a Hope for the Youth of Zion" (speech delivered at BYU).

"Our anxiety has been increased when we have listened to the attempts of men in high stations to stir up class hatreds that contradict the age-old constitutional guarantee of free enterprise."

Harold B. Lee

Donald Q. Cannon, Ed., 1991. *Latter-day Prophets and the United States Constitution* (Provo, Utah: Religious Studies Center, 1991), 144–55.

"There are several principles which undergird the significance of work in the Lord's plan. First, as the covenant people we must be as self-sufficient as possible. We are to be free from dependence upon a dole or any program that might endanger our free agency. Second, we must work to support the families with which the Lord has blessed us."

Howard W. Hunter

Howard W. Hunter, October 1975. "Prepare for Honorable Employment" (speech given at General Conference).

"I am unalterably opposed to Socialism, either in whole or in part, and regard it as an unconstitutional usurpation of power and a denial of the right of private property for government to own or operate the means of producing and distributing goods and services in competition with private enterprise, or to regiment owners in the legitimate use of private property."

Ezra Taft Benson

Ezra Taft Benson, 1969. "An Enemy Hath Done This," (Salt Lake City: Parliament Publishers).

"I should like to express gratitude . . . for this great country, for the Constitution of the United States which grants to each individual liberty, freedom to think and to speak and to act as he pleases, just so long as each gives to the other man that same privilege. I am thankful for this country which has given more persons opportunity to raise themselves under an individualistic, capitalistic, free enterprise system from menial to commanding positions than any other nation in the world, past or present."

David O. McKay

Donald Q. Cannon, Ed., *Latter-day Prophets and the United States Constitution* (Provo, Utah: Religious Studies Center, Brigham Young University, 1991), 116–33.

"Of all forms of incentive, the freedom to obtain a reward for ones labors is the most sustaining for most people, sometimes called the "profit motive". It is simply the right to plan and to earn, and to enjoy the fruits of your labor. This profit motive diminishes as government controls, regulations and taxes increase to deny the fruits of success to those who produce. Therefore any attempt through government intervention to redistribute the material rewards of labor can only result in the eventual destruction of the productive base of society, without which real abundance and security for more than the ruling elite is quite impossible."

Ezra Taft Benson

Ezra Taft Benson, *God, Family, Country: Our Three Great Loyalties* (Salt Lake City: Deseret Book Co., 1974) 295.

FROM THE SCRIPTURES:

"They altered their reckoning and their measure, according to the minds and the circumstances of the people, in every generation, until the reign of the judges, they having been established by king Mosiah. Now the reckoning is thus. . .a senum of silver was equal to a senine of gold, and either for a measure of barley . . . Now this is their number, according to their reckoning." *(A righteous leader simply regulated (made regular) the value of the money system and made it equal to a measurable quantity of a commodity. That is what the Founders gave Congress the power to do in Article I, Section 8, Clause 5)*

Alma 11:4-18

"And they did all labor, every man according to his strength. And they did impart of their substance, every man according to that which he had, to the poor, and the needy, and the sick, and the afflicted; . . . and now, because of the steadiness of the church they began to be exceedingly rich, having abundance of all things whatsoever they stood in need ... And thus, in their prosperous circumstances, they did not send away any who were naked, or that were hungry, or that were athirst, or that were sick, or that had not been nourished; and they did not set their hearts upon riches; therefore they were liberal to all, both old and young, both bond and free, both male and female, whether out of the church or in the church, having no respect to persons as to those who stood in need. And thus they did prosper and become far more wealthy than those who did not belong to their church." (True prosperity comes from working hard, not setting hearts on riches and by sharing liberally with all by choice, not by force.)

Alma 1:26-31

Freedom of Religion

From the Constitution:

"But no religious Test shall ever be required as a Qualification to any Office or public Trust under the United States."

Article VI, Clause 3

From the Founding Fathers:

"Well aware that the opinions and belief of men depend not on their own will, but follow involuntarily the evidence proposed to their minds; that Almighty God hath created the mind free, and manifested his supreme will that free it shall remain by making it altogether insusceptible of restraint; that all attempts to influence it by temporal punishments, or burthens, or by civil incapacitations, tend only to beget habits of hypocrisy and meanness, and are a departure from the plan of the holy author of our religion, who being lord both of body and mind, yet chose not to propagate it by coercions on either, as was in his Almighty power to do, but to extend it by its influence on reason alone; that the impious presumption of legislators and rulers, civil as well as ecclesiastical, who, being themselves but fallible and uninspired men, have assumed dominion over the faith of others, setting up their own opinions and modes of thinking as the only true and infallible, and as such endeavoring to impose them on others, hath established and maintained false religions over the greatest part of the world and through all time … no man shall be compelled to frequent or support any religious worship, place, or ministry whatsoever, nor shall be enforced, restrained, molested, or burthened in his body or goods, nor shall otherwise suffer, on account of his religious opinions or belief; but that all men shall be free to profess, and by argument to maintain, their opinions in matters of religion, and that the same shall in no wise diminish, enlarge, or affect their civil capacities."

Thomas Jefferson

Julian P. Boyd, Charles T. Cullen, John Catanzariti, Barbara B. Oberg, Eds., *The Papers of Thomas Jefferson, Vol. 2* (Princeton: Princeton University Press, 1950) 545-553.

FROM THE PROPHETS:

"When the Constitution of the United States was framed and adopted, those high contracting parties did positively agree that they would not interfere with religious affairs. Now, if our marital relations are not religious, what is? This ordinance of marriage was a direct revelation to us, through Joseph Smith, the prophet. . . . This is a revelation from God and a command to his people, and therefore it is my religion. I do not believe that the Supreme Court of the United States has any right to interfere with my religious views, and in doing it they are violating their most sacred obligations."

John Taylor

John Taylor "Popular History of Utah," (printed in The Deseret News, 1916), 318.

"In effect [the supreme court] has said that we may think as we please, but must not act. I would ask, in the name of the Lord, was that all Thomas Jefferson, and others had in their minds when they framed the clause in reference to religious liberty? What about men acting? If it was only intended that men should think and not act, why not say so in the instrument? Why should it be stated that 'Congress shall make no law respecting an establishment of religion, or prohibiting the free *exercise* thereof," if men were not to be allowed to act? Why, in the exercise of their religion, men must act ..."

Wilford Woodruff

John Henry Smith, *Journal of Discourses, Vol. 24* (Liverpool, 1884) 211.

"We do not expect that Congress is acquainted with our religious faith; but, as members of the body politic, we do claim the guarantees of the Constitution and immunity from persecution on merely religious grounds."

John Taylor

John Taylor, *Journal of Discourses, Vol. 11*, (Liverpool, 1867), 223.

"This is the doctrine of the Constitution, so help me God. The Constitution is not law to us, but it makes provision for us whereby we can make laws. Where it provides that no one shall be hindered from worshiping God according to his own conscience, is a law. No legislature can enact a law to prohibit it. The Constitution provides to regulate bodies of men and not individuals."

Joseph Smith

Joseph Fielding Smith, *Teachings of the Prophet Joseph Smith* (Salt Lake City: Deseret Book, 1977), 279.

"Every man is allowed by the Constitution to have what religion he pleases and to profess what religion he pleases. That liberty is guaranteed by the Constitution."

Brigham Young

Asa Calkin, *Brigham Young Journal of Discourses, Vol. 5* (Liverpool, 1858) 235.

"In this view we consider that the men of the Revolution were inspired by the Almighty, to throw off the shackles of the mother government, with her established religion. For this cause were Adams, Jefferson, Franklin, Washington, and a host of others inspired to deeds of resistance to the acts of the King of Great Britain, who might also have been led to those aggressive acts, for aught we know, to bring to pass the purposes of God in this establishing a new government upon a principle of greater freedom, a basis of self-government allowing the free exercise of religious worship."

Brigham Young

F.D. Richards, *Brigham Young Journal of Discourses, Vol. 2* (Liverpool, 1855) 170.

"I am bold to declare before Heaven that I am just as ready to die in defending the rights of a Presbyterian, a Baptist, or a good man of any other denomination [as for a Mormon]; for the same principle which would trample upon the rights of the Latter-day Saints would trample upon the rights of the Roman Catholics, or of any other denomination who may be unpopular and too weak to defend themselves. It is a love of liberty which inspires my soul—civil and religious liberty to the whole of the human race."

Joseph Smith

Asa Calkin, *Joseph Smith Latter-day Saints' Millennial Star, vol. 21* (Liverpool, 1859) 699.

FROM THE SCRIPTURES:

"We claim the privilege of worshiping Almighty God according to the dictates of our own conscience, and allow all menthe same privilege, let them worship how, where, or what they may."

11th Article of Faith

"Now there was no law against a man's belief; for it was strictly contrary to the commands of God that there should be a law which should bring men on to unequal grounds. For thus saith the scripture: Choose ye this day whom ye will serve. Now if a man desired to serve God, it was his privilege; or, rather, if he believed in God it was his privilege to serve him; but if he did not believe in him there was no law to punish him."

Alma 30:7-9

"For the freemen had sworn or covenanted to maintain their rights and the privileges of their religion by a free government."

Alma 51:6

"For they saw and beheld with great sorrow that the people of the church began to be lifted up in the pride of their eyes, and to set their hearts upon riches and upon the vain things of the world, that they began to be scornful, one towards another, and *they began to persecute those that did not believe according to their own will and pleasure*."

Alma 4:8

GOD'S CENTRAL ROLE

FROM THE CONSTITUTION:

Legislative: "The Laws of Nature and of Nature's God", "All men are created equal, that they are endowed by their Creator with certain unalienable Rights" *(God is the great Lawgiver of the Universe)*

Executive: "With a firm reliance on the protection of divine Providence." *(God is the great Protector and Executor of the Universe)*

Judicial: "Appealing to the Supreme Judge of the world." *(God is the great Judge of the Universe)*

Declaration of Indenpendence

FROM THE FOUNDING FATHERS:

"Only a virtuous people are capable of freedom. As nations become corrupt and vicious, they have more need of masters."

Benjamin Franklin

John Bigelow, Ed., *The Works of Benjamin Franklin, Vol. 11* (New York: G.P. Putnam's Sons, 1904) 318.

"Neither the wisest constitution nor the wisest laws will secure the liberty and happiness of a people whose manners are universally corrupt. He therefore is the truest friend to the liberty of his country who tries most to promote its virtue, and who ... will not suffer a man to be chosen into any office of power and trust who is not a wise and virtuous man."

Samuel Adams

William Vincent Wells, *The Life and Public Services of Samuel Adams* (Boston: Little, Brown, and Co., 1865) 22.

"Those rights, then, which God and nature have established, and are therefore called natural rights, such as are life and liberty, need not the aid of human laws to be more effectually invested in every man than they are; neither do they receive any additional strength when declared by the municipal [or state] laws to be inviolable. On the contrary, no human legislation has power to abridge or destroy them, unless the owner [of the right] shall himself commit some act that amounts to a forfeiture."

William Blackstone *(not a founding father, but a great quote)*

A. Strahan, *Commentaries on the Laws of England, Vol. 1* (London, 1803) 54.

"Rights are not gifts from one man to another, nor from one class of men to another... It is impossible to discover any origin of rights otherwise than in the origin of man; it consequently follows that rights appertain to man in right of his existence, and must therefore be equal to every man."

Thomas Paine

Moncure Daniel Conway, Ed., *The Writings of Thomas Paine, Vol. 3*, (New York: G.P.Putnam's Sons, 1895), 271.

"Can the liberties of a nation be thought secure when we have removed their only firm basis, a conviction in the minds of the people that these liberties are the gift of God? That they are not be violated but with his wrath? Indeed I tremble for my country when I reflect that God is just: that his justice cannot sleep for ever."

Thomas Jefferson

Ford Paul Leicester, ed., *The Writings of Thomas Jefferson, Vol. 4* (New York: G.P. Putnam's Sons, 1892-99), 232.

"All eyes are opened, or opening, to the rights of man. The general spread of the light of science has already laid open to every view the palpable truth, that the mass of mankind has not been born with saddles on their backs, nor a favored few booted and spurred, ready to ride them legitimately, by the grace of God. These are grounds of hope for others. For ourselves, let the annual return of this day forever refresh our recollections of these rights, and an undiminished devotion to them."

Thomas Jefferson

Andrew A. Lipscomb and Albert Ellery Bergh, Ed., *The Writings of Thomas Jefferson, Vol. 16* (Washington: Thomas Jefferson Memorial Association, 1905), 182.

"Equal laws protecting equal rights — the best guarantee of loyalty and love of country."

James Madison

Gaillard Hunt, Ed., *The Writings of James Madison, Vol. 9* (Letter to Jacob de la Motta written in 1820) 30.

"Of all the dispositions and habits which lead to political prosperity, religion and morality are indispensable supports. In vain would that man claim the tribute of patriotism, who should labor to subvert these great pillars of human happiness, these firmest props of the duties of men and citizens. The mere politician, equally with the pious man, ought to respect and to cherish them. A volume could not trace all their connections with private and public felicity. Let it simply be asked: Where is the security for property, for reputation, for life, if the sense of religious obligation desert the oaths which are the instruments of investigation in courts of justice? And let us with caution indulge the supposition that morality can be maintained without religion. Whatever may be conceded to the influence of refined education on minds of peculiar structure, reason and experience both forbid us to expect that national morality can prevail in exclusion of religious principle."

George Washington

Charles W. Dunn, Ed., "George Washington 1796 Farewell Address," *The Future of Religion in American Politics* (Lexington: University Press of Kentucky, 2009), 104.

The following quotes do not necessarily support the idea of God's central role in government but they do provide interesting insights into some of the Founders' religious beliefs.

"Here is my Creed. I believe in one God, Creator of the Universe: That he governs the World by his Providence. That he ought to be worshipped. That the most acceptable Service we can render to him is doing good to his other Children. That the Soul of Man is immortal, and will be treated with Justice in another Life respecting its Conduct in this. These I take to be the fundamental Principles of all sound Religion, and I regard them as you do in whatever Sect I meet with them."

Benjamin Franklin

Franklin Bowditch Dexter, *The Literary Diary of Ezra Stiles, Vol. 3* (New York: Scribner's Sons, 1901), 387.

"I have now disposed of all my property to my family. There is one thing more I wish I could give them, and that is the Christian Religion. If they had that and I had not given them one shilling they would have been rich; and if they had not that and I had given them all the world, they would be poor."

Patrick Henry

Johnstone and Hunter, *The Christian Treasury, Vol. 5* (Edinburgh, 1801), 130.

"To the corruptions of Christianity I am, indeed opposed; but not to the genuine precepts of Jesus himself. I am a Christian, in the only sense in which he wished any one to be; sincerely attached to his doctrines, in preference to all others."

Thomas Jefferson

Andrew A. Lipscomb and Albert E. Bergh, Eds., *The Writings of Thomas Jefferson. Vol. 10* (Washington, D.C.: Thomas Jefferson Memorial Association of the United States, 1903-04), 380.

"No one sees with greater pleasure than myself the progress of reason in it's advances towards rational Christianity. when we shall have done away the incomprehensible jargon of the Trinitarian arithmetic, that three are one, and one is three; when we shall have knocked down the artificial scaffolding, reared to mask from view the simple structure of Jesus, when, in short, we shall have unlearned every thing which has been taught since his day, and got back to the pure and simple doctrines he inculcated, we shall then be truly and worthily his disciples: and my opinion is that if nothing had ever been added to what flowed purely from his lips, the whole world would at this day have been

Christian ...I do not wish to trouble the world with mine, nor to be troubled for them. these accounts are to be settled only with him who made us; and to him we leave it, with charity for all others, of whom also he is the only rightful and competent judge. I have little doubt that the whole of our country will soon be rallied to the Unity of the Creator, and, I hope, to the pure doctrines of Jesus also."

Thomas Jefferson

Dickinson W. Adams and Ruth W. Lester, eds. *Jefferson's Extracts from the Gospels: "The Philosophy of Jesus" and "The Life and Morals of Jesus"* (Princeton: Princeton University Press, 1983), 403.

FROM THE PROPHETS:

"Hence we say, that the Constitution of the United States is a glorious standard; it is founded in the wisdom of God. It is a heavenly banner; it is to all those who are privileged with the sweets of liberty, like the cooling shades and refreshing waters of a great rock in a thirsty and weary land. It is like a great tree under whose branches men from every clime can be shielded from the burning rays of the sun...We say that God is true; that the Constitution of the United States is true; that the Bible is true; that the Book of Mormon is true ..."

Joseph Smith

Joseph F. Smith, *Teachings of the Prophet Joseph Smith* (Salt Lake City: Deseret Book, 1977) 147-148.

"[One] principle that actuated the lives of the fathers who founded our Constitution was faith in God."

David O. McKay

Donald Q. Cannon, ed., *Latter-day Prophets and the United States Constitution* (Provo, Utah: Religious Studies Center, Brigham Young University, 1991), 116-33.

"So the perpetuity of this land and nation depends upon faith. Any power or any influence that will destroy directly or indirectly this principle of faith in God is an enemy to the Constitution of the United States."

David O. McKay

Donald Q. Cannon, ed., *Latter-day Prophets and the United States Constitution* (Provo, Utah: Religious Studies Center, Brigham Young University, 1991), 116-33.

"I would to God that the rulers of our land—the President of the United States, the Congress of the United States, the Supreme Court of the United States—would learn the responsibility the God of heaven will hold them to in the administration of those glorious principles laid down in the Constitution of the government of this country."

-Wilford Woodruff

John Henry Smith, *Wilford Woodruff Journal of Discourses, vol. 24* (Liverpool, 1884) 11.

"We trace the hand of the Almighty in framing the constitution of our land, and believe that the Lord raised up men purposely for the accomplishment of this object, raised them up and inspired them to frame the constitution of the United States."

Lorenzo Snow

Horace S. Edlredge, *Lorenzo Snow Journal of Discourses, vol. 13* (Liverpool, 1871) 301.

"Now, these are the commandments of God, the principles contained in these commandments of the great Eternal are the principles that underlie the Constitution of our country and all just laws."

Joseph F. Smith

Donald Q. Cannon, Ed., *Latter-day Prophets and the United States Constitution,* (Provo, Utah: Religious Studies Center, Brigham Young University, 1991), 84-90.

"I pray that America may always be worthy of [God's] blessing. There is no place for arrogance among us. There is no place for conceit or egotism. As we look to God, we will grow in strength."

Gordon B. Hinckley

Gordon B. Hinckley, 1996. Speech at the Salt Lake LDS Tabernacle during the American Legion's 78th National Convention.

"Besides the preaching of the Gospel, we have another mission, namely, the perpetuation of the free agency of man and the maintenance of liberty, freedom, and the rights of man. There are certain principles that belong to humanity outside of the Constitution, outside of the laws, outside of all the enactments and plans of man, among which is the right to live; God gave us the right and not man; no government gave it to us, and no government has a right to take it away from us. We have a right to liberty—that was a right that God gave to all men; and if there has been oppression, fraud or tyranny in the earth, it has been the result of the wickedness and corruptions of men and has always been opposed to God and the principles of truth, righteousness, virtue, and all principles that are calculated to elevate mankind. The Declaration of Independence states that men are in possession of certain inalienable rights, among which are life, liberty and the pursuit of happiness. This belongs to us; it belongs to all humanity. I wish, and the worst wish I have for the United States, is, that they could have liberality enough to give to all men equal rights."

John Taylor

John Henry Smith, *John Taylor Journal of Discourses, vol. 23* (Liverpool, 1883) 63.

From the Scriptures:

"And now, we can behold the decrees of God concerning this land, that it is a land of promise; and whatsoever nation shall possess it shall serve God, or they shall be swept off when the fulness of his wrath shall come upon them. And the fulness of his wrath cometh upon them when they are ripened in iniquity. For behold, this is a land which is choice above all other lands; wherefore he that doth possess it shall serve God or shall be swept off; for it is the everlasting decree of God."

Ether 2:9-10

"Wherefore, this land is consecrated unto him whom he shall bring. And if it so be that they shall serve him according to the commandments which he hath given, it shall be a land of liberty unto them; wherefore, they shall never be brought down into captivity; if so, it shall be because of iniquity; for if iniquity shall abound cursed shall be the land for their sakes, but unto the righteous it shall be blessed forever."

2 Nephi 1:7

"According to the Spirit of God, which is also the spirit of freedom."

Alma 61:15

"Amalickiah . . . led away the hearts of many people to do wickedly; yea, and to seek to destroy the church of God, and to destroy the foundation of liberty which God had granted unto them, or which blessing God had sent upon the face of the land for the righteous' sake."

Alma 46:10

"Where the Spirit of the Lord is, there is liberty"

2 Corinthians 3:17

"Let no man break the laws of the land, for he that keepeth the laws of God hath no need to break the laws of the land."

Doctrine and Covenants 58:21

"There is a law, irrevocably decreed in heaven before the foundations of this world, upon which all blessings are predicated–and when we obtain any blessing from God, it is by obedience to that law upon which it is predicated."

Doctrine and Covenants 130:20-21

Natural Law

An analysis of God's central role doesn't seem complete without looking at natural laws – God's laws – and exploring the supporting statements from founders and prophets regarding it.

From the Prophets:

"It is hard to get the people to believe that God is a scientific character, that He lives by Science or strict law, that by this He is, and by Law He was made what He is; and will remain to all eternity because of His faithful adherence to law. It is a most difficult thing to make the people believe that every Art and Science and all Wisdom comes from Him, and that He is their Author."

Brigham Young

Fred C. Collier, *Brigham Young's Doctrine on Deity or Adam-God, Vol. 1* (Collier Publishing Co.) 139-140.

"True science is a discovery of the secret, immutable and eternal laws, by which the universe is governed; and when practically applied, sets in motion the mighty wheels of useful engines, with all the various machinery which genius has invented, or art contrived. –It ameliorates the condition of man, by extending the means of intellectual, moral, social, and domestic happiness."

John Taylor

Taylor and Woodruff, Ed., *The Times and Seasons Vol. 4*, (Nauvoo, 1863), 46.

"There is no being in all the eternities but what is governed by law."

Brigham Young

Albert Carrington, *Brigham Young Journal of Discourses, Vol. 14* (Liverpool, 1872), 280.

FROM THE SCRIPTURES:

"Yea, and all things denote there is a God; yea, even the earth, and all things that are upon the face of it, yea, and its motion, yea, and also all the planets which move in their regular form do witness that there is a Supreme Creator."

Alma 30:44

"I perceive that it has been made known unto you, by the testimony of his word, that he cannot walk in crooked paths; neither doth he vary from that which he hath said; neither hath he a shadow of turning from the right to the left, or from that which is right to that which is wrong; therefore, his course is one eternal round."

Alma 7:20

"Yea, even ye have received all things, both things in heaven, and all things which are in the earth, as a witness that they are true."

Helaman 8:24

"And again, verily I say unto you, that which is governed by law is also preserved by law and perfected and sanctified by the same. That which breaketh a law, and abideth not by law, but seeketh to become a law unto itself, and willeth to abide in sin, and altogether abideth in sin, cannot be sanctified by law, neither by mercy, justice nor judgment. Therefore, they must remain filthy still. All kingdoms have a law given... and unto every kingdom is given a law; and unto every law there are certain bounds also and conditions. All beings who abide not in those conditions are not justified... judgment goeth before the face of him who sitteth upon the throne and governeth and executeth all things. He comprehendeth all things, and all things are before him... he hath give a law unto all things, by which they move in their times and their seasons; and their courses are fixed, even the courses of the heavens and the earth and all the planets. And they give light to each other in their times and in their seasons."

Doctrine and Covenants 88:34-39

INDIVIDUAL AGENCY

FROM THE CONSTITUTION:

"The powers not delegated to the United States by the Constitution, nor prohibited by it to the States, are reserved to the States respectively, or to the people."

10th Amendment

"No state shall . . . grant any Title of Nobility."

Article I, Section 10, Clause 1

"The right of the people to be secure in their persons, houses, papers and effects, against unreasonable searches and seizures, shall not be violated, and no Warrants shall issue, but upon probable cause, supported by Oath or affirmation, and particularly describing the place to be searched, and the persons or things to be seized.

4th Amendment

"In all criminal prosecutions, the accused shall enjoy the right to a speedy and public trial, by an impartial jury . . . and to be informed of the nature and cause of the accusation; to be confronted with the witnesses against him; to have compulsory process for obtaining witnesses in his favor, and to have the assistance of counsel for his defence." (The presumption of innocence of the individual and protections to help against invasion of his rights)

6th Amendment

FROM THE FOUNDING FATHERS:

"Of liberty then I would say that, in the whole plenitude of its extent, it is unobstructed action according to our will. But rightful liberty is unobstructed action according to our will, within the limits drawn around us by the equal rights of others. I do not add 'within the limits of the law,' because law is often but the tyrant's will and always so when it violates the right of an individual. "

Thomas Jefferson

Joyce Appleby and Terence Ball, ed., *Jefferson: Political Writings* (New York: Cambridge University Press, 1999), 224.

"The fabric of American empire ought to rest on the solid basis of the consent of the people. The streams of national power ought to flow immediately from that pure, original fountain of all legislative authority."

Alexander Hamilton

Alexander Hamilton, *The Federalist Papers #22* (New York : Cosimo Classics, 2006), 141.

"If a nation expects to be ignorant and free, in a state of civilization, it expects what never was and never will be."

Thomas Jefferson

Paul Leicester Ford, *The Works of Thomas Jefferson, Federal Edition, Vol. 11* (New York and London: G.P. Putnam's Sons, 1904-5) 498

"I know no safe depository of the ultimate powers of the society but the people themselves; and if we think them not enlightened enough to exercise their control with a wholesome discretion, the remedy is not to take it from them, but to inform their discretion by education. This is the true corrective of abuses of constitutional power."

Thomas Jefferson

Paul Leicester Ford, *The Works of Thomas Jefferson, Federal Edition, Vol. 12* (New York and London: G.P. Putnam's Sons, 1904-5), 163.

From the Prophets:

"Efforts are being made to deprive man of his free agency, to steal from the individual his liberty; and we must never forget that next to life itself, free agency is the greatest gift of God man. ... We know, also, that there has been an alarming increase in the abandoning of the ideals that constitute the foundation of the Constitution of the United States."

David. O. McKay

David O. McKay *Conference Report October 1966* (SLC: The Church of Jesus Christ of Latter-day Saints), 4-8.

"The Constitution of the United States, as given to us by our fathers, is the real government under which individuals may exercise free agency and individual initiative."

David O. McKay

Donald Q. Cannon, ed., *Latter-day Prophets and the United States Constitution* (Utah: Religious Studies Center, Brigham Young University, 1991), 116–33.

"Another fundamental for which we should be grateful is the free agency which God has given us – freedom and liberty vouchsafed by the Constitution of the United States. I wonder if we appreciate this great gift. That free agency, the right to exercise that free agency, and the right of trial by your equals is vouchsafed by the Constitution of the United States. Let us have a spirit of gratitude in our hearts for the free exercise of our agency and the rights of liberty."

David O. McKay

Donald Q. Cannon, ed., *Latter-day Prophets and the United States Constitution* (Utah: Religious Studies Center, Brigham Young University, 1991), 116–33.

"If man will not recognize the inequalities around him and voluntarily, through the gospel plan, come to the aid of his brother, he will find that through "a democratic process" he will be forced to come to the aid of his brother. The government will take from the "haves" and give to the "have nots." Both have last their freedom. Those who "have," lost their freedom to give voluntarily of their own free will and in the way they desire. Those who "have not," lost their freedom because they did not earn what they received. They got "something for nothing," and they will neither appreciate the gift nor the giver of the gift. Under this climate, people become blind to what has happened and to the vital freedoms which they have lost."

Howard W. Hunter

Howard W. Hunter, 1966. "The Law of the Harvest" (Devotional address at Brigham Young University), 1-11.

"It is the right of every soul to have equal and unrestricted justice before the law, equal rights to worship according to the dictates of conscience and to labor according to the individual inclinations, independently of coercion or compulsion."

Joseph Fielding Smith.

Joseph Fielding Smith, *Doctrines of Salvation: Sermons and Writings* (SLC: Bookcraft, 1973), 325.

"Next to the divine authority of the Priesthood I believe that no principle of the Gospel is more endangered today than is that principle which gives us individual freedom...It was that very principle that induced our Founding Fathers to declare their independence from the countries in Europe and to establish the Constitution, giving to each individual the right to worship, the right to build, the right to work, the right to think, to speak, to preach, so long as each gave to other individuals that same privilege."

David O. McKay

Donald Q. Cannon, ed., *Latter-day Prophets and the United States Constitution* (Utah: Religious Studies Center, Brigham Young University, 1991), 116–33.

"And if the people have given up to governors, legislatures, the judiciary and to the officers of the law certain powers, rights and privileges, this authority coming of or from the people, it is expected that they shall act for and in the interests of the people; and furthermore, that while they possess those rights ceded to them by the people, whatever is not thus ceded and placed in the hands of their rulers is emphatically stated to be reserved to the several States or to the people. . . But it must be understood here in matters pertaining to our government, that no charters or grants of any kind can be given by any parties, in excess of the rights which they themselves possess, and that the same obligations which vest in regard to constitutional rights and guarantees must be observed in all those municipal regulations by the recipients as of the grantees of those charters.

These rights and privileges in our government are formulated upon the idea that our government is 'of the people, by the people and for the people.'"

John Taylor

Daniel H. Wells, *Journal of Discourses, Vol. 26* (Liverpool, 1886), 349.

"I suppose it is thought by a great many that we ought to consider it a great privilege to be allowed to live. We do think so, but we are not indebted to any officials for it; they did not give us our life, neither did this government. There are certain principles that are inherent in man, that belong to man, and that were enunciated in an early day, before the United States government was formed, and they are principles that rightfully belong to all men everywhere. They are described in the Declaration of Independence as inalienable rights, one of which is that men have a right to live; another is that they have a right to pursue happiness; and another is that they have a right to be free and no man has authority to deprive them of those God-given rights, and none but tyrants would do it. These principles I say, are inalienable in man; they belong to him; they existed before any constitutions were framed or any laws made."

John Taylor

John Henry Smith, *Journal of Discourses, Vol. 23* (Liverpool, 1883), 263.

"Actuated by these two fundamental and eternal principles – the free agency of the individual and faith in an overruling Providence – those 56 men who signed the Declaration of Independence, those who drew up the Constitution of the United States nine years later, gave to the world a concept of government which, if applied, will strike from the arms of downtrodden humanity the shackles of tyranny, and give hope, ambition, and freedom to the teeming millions throughout the world."

David O. McKay

Donald Q. Cannon, ed., *Latter-day Prophets and the United States Constitution* (Utah: Religious Studies Center, Brigham Young University, 1991), 116–33.

"The honorable framers of the Constitution of the United States were no less alive to these matters, and while they threw safeguards around the civil power, [they] were very anxious to protect the people in their individual, social, religious and political rights."

John Taylor

A. Carrington, *The Latter-day Saints' Millennial Star, Vol. 33* (Liverpool, 1871) 739.

"Your constitution guarantees to every citizen, even the humblest, the enjoyment of life, liberty, and property. It promises to all, religious freedom, the right to all to worship God beneath their own vine and fig tree, according to the dictates of their conscience. It guarantees to all the citizens of the several states the right to become citizens of any one of the states, and to enjoy all the rights and immunities of the citizens of the state of his adoption."

Joseph Smith

George Q. Cannon, *The Life of Joseph Smith, the Prophet, Juvenile Instructor Office* (Salt Lake City, 1888), 303.

FROM THE SCRIPTURES:

"And he told them that these things ought not to be; but that the burden should come upon all the people, that every man might bear his part . . . and [they] became exceedingly anxious that every man should have an equal chance throughout all the land; yea, and every man expressed a willingness to answer for his own sins."

Mosiah 29:34, 38

"Wherefore, because that Satan rebelled against me, and sought to destroy the agency of man, which I, the Lord God, had given him, and also, that I should give unto him mine own power; by the power of mine Only Begotten, I caused that he should be cast down."

Moses 4:3

"And all men are instructed sufficiently that they may know good from evil. And the law is given unto men... For it must needs be that there is an opposition in all things. If not...righteousness could not be brought to pass, neither wickedness, neither holiness nor misery, neither good nor bad. Wherefore, all things must needs be compound in one; ... Wherefore, it must needs have been created for a thing of naught; wherefore there would have been no purpose in the end of its creation ... neither to act nor to be acted upon... There is a God, and he hath created all things... both things to act and things to be acted upon... they have become free forever, knowing good from evil; to act for themselves and not to be acted upon, save it be by the punishment of the law at the great and last day, according to the commandments which God hath given. Wherefore, men are free according to the flesh; and all things are given them which are expedient unto man. And they are free to choose liberty and eternal life, through the great Mediator of all men, or to choose captivity and death, according to the captivity and power of the devil; for he seeketh that all men might be miserable like unto himself."

2 Nephi 2:5, 11-13, 26-27

"And now remember, remember, my brethren, that whosoever perisheth, perisheth unto himself; and whosoever doeth iniquity, doeth it unto himself; for behold, ye are free; ye are permitted to act for yourselves; for behold, God hath given unto you a knowledge and he hath made you free."

Helaman 14:30

"And truth is knowledge of things as they are, and as they were, and as they are to come; . . . All truth is independent in that sphere in which God has placed it, to act for itself, as all intelligence also; otherwise there is no existence. Behold, here is the agency of man."

Doctrine and Covenants 93:24, 30-31

LIMITED POWER

FROM THE CONSTITUTION:

"All legislative Powers *herein granted.*" (Only certain powers are granted to government)

Article I, Section 1, Clause 1

"This Constitution, and the Laws of the United States *which shall be made in Pursuance thereof* ... shall be the supreme Law of the Land." (Notice, not all federal laws are supreme. Only those that meet the condition of following, or pursuing, the Constitution).

Article VI, Clause 2

"All Treaties made, or which shall be made, under the Authority of the United States, shall be the supreme Law of the Land." (Notice, only treaties that are made *under the authority of the United States* – which authority is granted in the Constitution – are the supreme law of the land)

Article VI, Clause 2

"[The Congress shall have Power] to make all laws which shall be necessary and proper *for carrying into Execution the foregoing Powers.*"

Article I, Section 8, Clause 18

Author's Note: *This is not a blank check to make whatever laws are subjectively deemed 'necessary and proper' by Congress. Rather, this is a grant of power to make laws which are necessary and proper in order to bring to pass the specific listed powers of article I, Section 8.*

"The powers not delegated to the United States by the Constitution, nor prohibited by it to the States, are reserved to the States respectively, or to the people."

10th Amendment

"The enumeration in the Constitution, of certain rights, shall not be construed to deny or disparage others retained by the people."

9th Amendment

"That to secure these rights Governments are instituted among Men."

Declaration of Independence

FROM THE FOUNDING FATHERS:

"It is weakness rather than wickedness which renders men unfit to be trusted with unlimited power."

John Adams

Budd and Bartram, *A Defence of the Constitutions of Government of the United States of America* (Philadelphia, 1797), 129.

The following statements are made in defense of the idea that the general welfare clause is an introductory, limiting statement

"Nothing is more natural nor common than first to use a general phrase, and then to explain and qualify it by a recital of particulars."

James Madison

James Madison, *The Federalist Papers #41* (New York : Cosimo Classics, 2006), 269.

"Our tenet ever was...that Congress had not unlimited powers to provide for the general welfare, but were restrained to those specifically enumerated, and that, as it was never meant that they should provide for that welfare but by the exercise of the enumerated powers, so it could not have been meant they should raise money for purposes which the enumeration did not place under their action; consequently, that the specification of powers is a limitation of the purposes for which they may raise money."

Thomas Jefferson

Philip B. Kurland and Thomas Lerner, ed., *The Founders' Constitution, Vol. 2* (University of Chicago Press, 2000), 425.

"The powers of the federal government are enumerated; it can only operate in certain cases; it has legislative powers on defined and limited objects, beyond which it cannot extend its jurisdiction."

James Madison

Frank Moore, *American Eloquence: A Collection of Speeches and Addresses, Vol. 1* (New York: D. Appleton and Co., 1880), 131.

"To take a single step beyond the boundaries thus specially drawn around the powers of Congress, is to take possession of a boundless field of power not longer susceptible of any definition."

Thomas Jefferson

Jefferson Powell, *A Community Built on Words: The Constitution in History and Politics* (University of Chicago Press, 2005), 27.

"If Congress can do whatever in their discretion can be done by money, and will promote the General Welfare, the Government is no longer a limited one, possessing enumerated powers, but an indefinite one, subject to particular exceptions."

James Madison

John Curtis Samples, *James Madison and the Future of Limited Government* (Washington D.C.: CATO Institute, 2002), 34.

"Money cannot be applied to the general welfare otherwise than by an application of it to some particular measures, conducive to the general welfare. Whenever, therefore, money has been raised by the general authority, and is to be applied to a particular measure, a question arises whether the particular measure be within the enumerated authorities vested in Congress. If it be, the money requisite for it may be applied to it; if it be not, no such application can be made."

James Madison

John Curtis Samples, *James Madison and the Future of Limited Government* (Washington D.C.: CATO Institute, 2002), 34.

The following two quotes come from Frédéric *Bastiat who wrote an incredibly simple, logical and powerful treatise on freedom called, The Law. Of course, I couldn't copy and paste the book in its entirety but I highly recommend reading it.*

"We hold from God the gift which includes all others. This gift is life – physical, intellectual, and moral life.

"But life cannot maintain itself alone. The Creator of life has entrusted us with the responsibility of preserving, developing, and perfecting it. In order that we may accomplish this, He has provided us with a collection of marvelous faculties. And He has put us in the midst of a variety of natural resources. By the application of our faculties to these natural resources we convert them into products, and use them. This process is necessary in order that life may run its appointed course.

"Life, faculties, production – in other words, individuality, liberty, property – this is man. And in spite of the cunning of artful political leaders, these three gifts from God precede all human legislation, and are superior to it.

"Life, liberty and property do not exist because men have made laws. On the contrary, it was the fact that life, liberty and property existed beforehand that caused men to make laws in the first place. …

"What, then, is law? It is the collective organization of the individual right to lawful defense.

"Each of us has a natural right – from God – to defend his person, his liberty, and his property. These are the three basic requirements of life, and the preservation of any one of them is completely dependent upon the preservation of the other two. For what are our faculties but the extension of our individuality? And what is property but an extension of our faculties?

"If every person has the right to defend – even by force – his person, his liberty, and his property, then it follows that a group of men have the right to organize and support a common force to protect these rights constantly. Thus the principle of collective right – its reason for existing, its lawfulness – is based on individual right. And the common force that protects this collective right cannot logically have any other purpose or any other mission than that for which it acts as a substitute. Thus, since an individual cannot lawfully use force against the person, liberty, or property of another individual, then the common force – for the same reason – cannot lawfully be used to destroy the person, liberty, or property of individuals or groups.

"Such a perversion of force would be, in both cases, contrary to our premise. Force has been given to us to defend our own individual rights. Who will dare to say that force has been given to us to destroy the equal rights of our brothers? Since no individual acting separately can lawfully use force to destroy the rights of others, does it not logically follow that the same principle also applies to the common force that is nothing more than the organized combination of the individual forces?

"If this is true, then nothing can be more evident than this: The law is the organization of the natural right of lawful defense. It is the substitution of a common force for individual forces. And this common force is to do only what the individual forces have a natural and lawful right to do: to protect persons, liberties, and properties; to maintain the right of each, and to cause justice to reign over us all."

Frédéric Bastiat *(not a founding father, but a great quote)*

Frédéric Bastiat, *The Law*, (New York: Cosimo Classics, 2006), 5-6.

"It seems to me that the rights of the state can be nothing but the regularizing of pre-existent personal rights. For my part, I cannot conceive a collective right that does not have its foundation in an individual right or presuppose it. Hence, to know whether the state is legitimately invested with a right, we must ask whether the individual has that right in virtue of his nature and in the absence of all government."

Frédéric Bastiat *(not a founding father, but a great quote)*

Seymour Cain, ed., *Selected Essays on Political Economy* (1995), 211.

FROM THE PROPHETS:

"We believe that all legislative assemblies should confine themselves to constitutional principles; and that all such laws should be implicitly obeyed by every American."

John Taylor

Donald Q. Cannon, ed., *John Taylor in Latter-day Prophets and the United States Constitution* (Provo, Utah: Religious Studies Center, Brigham Young University, 1991), 36–69.

"The Constitution acknowledges that the people have all power not reserved to itself...This is the doctrine of the Constitution, so help me God. The Constitution provides to regulate bodies of men and not individuals."

Joseph Smith

Joseph Fielding Smith, *Teachings of the Prophet Joseph Smith* (Salt Lake City: Deseret Book, 1977), 279.

"All laws that are proper and correct, and all obligations entered into which are not violative of the constitution should be kept inviolate. But if they are violative of the constitution, then the compact between the rulers and the ruled is broken and the obligation ceases to be binding. Just as a person agreeing to purchase anything and to pay a certain amount for it, if he receives the article bargained for, and does not pay its price, he violates his contract; but if he does not receive the article he is not required to pay for it."

John Taylor

Daniel H. Wells, *John Taylor Journal of Discourses, Vol. 26* (Liverpool, 1886), 350.

FROM THE SCRIPTURES:

"Nevertheless, they durst not lie, if it were known, for fear of the law, for liars were punished; therefore they pretended to preach according to their belief; and now the law could have no power on any man for his belief. And they durst not steal, for fear of the law, for such were punished; neither durst they rob, nor murder, for he that murdered was punished unto death"

Alma 1:17-18

"No power or influence can or ought to be maintained by virtue of the priesthood, only by persuasion, by long suffering, by gentleness and meekness and by love unfeigned; . . . then shall thy confidence wax strong in the presence of God; and the doctrine of the priesthood shall distill upon thy soul as the dews from heaven. . . . and thy scepter an unchanging scepter of righteousness and truth; and thy dominion shall be an everlasting dominion and without compulsory means it shall flow unto thee forever and ever.

Doctrine and Covenants 121:41-46

Author's Note: *Since God's government is the priesthood, if you substitute the word "government" for the words "the priesthood" there are great lessons to be learned.*

Private Property

From the Constitution:

"No Capitation, or other direct, Tax shall be laid, unless in Proportion to the Census or Enumeration herein before directed to be taken."

Article I, Section 9, Clause 4

Author's Note: *No direct tax unless everyone is taxed the same to pay for a governmental action that benefits all*

"All Duties, Imposts and Excises shall be uniform throughout the United States."

Article I, Section 8, Clause 1

Author's Note: *Indirect taxes were to be equally applied to the exchange of property of the people so as to not favor one citizen's property over another's.*

"No state shall . . . pass any . . . Law impairing the Obligation of Contracts."

Article I, Section 10, Clause 1

"[The Congress shall have Power] to promote the Progress of Science and useful Arts, by securing for limited Times to Authors and Inventors the exclusive Right to their respective Writings and Discoveries"

Article I, Section 8, Clause 8

From the Founding Fathers:

"[Property] in its particular application means 'that dominion which one man claims and exercises over the external things of the world, in exclusion of every other individual.' In its larger and juster meaning, it embraces every thing to which a man may attach a value and have a right; and which leaves to every one else the like advantage. In the former sense, a man's land, or merchandize, or money is called his property. In the latter sense, a man has a property in his opinions and the free communication of them. He has a property of peculiar value in his religious opinions, and in the profession and practice dictated by them. He has a property very dear to him in the safety and liberty of his person. He has an equal property in the free use of his faculties and free choice of the objects on which to employ them. In a word, as a man is said to have a right to his property, he may be equally said to have a property in his rights."

James Madison

Gaillard Hunt, ed., *The Writings of James Madison Vol. 6*, (New York: G.P. Putnam's Sons, 1900), 101.

"The great and chief end, therefore, of men's uniting . . . and putting themselves under government, is the preservation of their property."

John Locke (not a founding father, but a great quote)

John Locke, *Two Treatises on Government, Bettesworth, Pemberton and Symon* (London, 1728), 226.

"Every Man has a Property in his own Person; This no body has any Right to but himself. The Labour of his Body, and the Work of his Hands, we may say, are properly his. Whatsoever then he removes out of the State that Nature hath provided, and left it in, he hath mixed his Labour with, and joined to it something that is his own, and thereby makes it his Property"

John Locke (not a founding father, but a great quote)

Bettesworth, Pemberton and Symon, *Two Treatises on Government* (London, 1728), 160-161.

"The utopian schemes of levelling, and a community of goods, are as visionary and impracticable, as those which vest all property in the Crown, are arbitrary, despotic, and, in our government unconstitutional."

Samuel Adams

Harry Alonzo Cushing, ed., *The Writings of Samuel Adams, Vol. 1* (New York: G.P. Putnam's Sons, 1904) 137.

FROM THE PROPHETS:

"The civil government's obligation then is to safeguard this right and to frame laws which secure to every man the free exercise of his conscience and the right and control of his property. No liberty is possible except a man is protected in his title to his legal holdings and property and can be indemnified by the law for its loss or destruction. Remove this right and man is reduced to serfdom. Former United States Supreme Court Justice George Southerland said it this way. 'To give man liberty but take from him the property which is the fruit and badge of his liberty is to still leave him a slave.'"

Ezra Taft Benson

Ezra Taft Benson, *The Teachings of Ezra Taft Benson* (SLC: Bookcraft, 1988), 608.

"To enter the United Order, when it was being tried, one consecrated all his possessions to the Church by a "covenant and a deed which" could not "be broken." (Doctrine and Covenants 42:30.) That is, he completely divested himself of all of his property by conveying it to the Church. Having thus voluntarily divested himself of title to all his property, the consecrator received from the Church a stewardship by a like conveyance. This stewardship could be more or less than his original consecration, the object being to make "every man equal according to his family, according to his circumstances and his wants and needs." (Doctrine and Covenants 51:3.) This procedure preserved in every man the right to private ownership and management of his property. At his own option he could alienate it or keep and operate it and pass it on to his heirs. The intent was, however, for him to so operate his property as to produce a living for himself and his dependents. So long as he remained in the order, he consecrated to the Church the surplus he produced above the needs and wants of his family. This surplus went into a storehouse from which stewardships were given to others and from which the needs of the poor were supplied. . . . the United Order is operated upon the principle of private ownership and individual management."

Marion G. Romney

Marion G. Romney, *Conference Report April 1966* (SLC: The Church of Jesus Christ of Latter-day Saints), 95-101.

"I am unalterably opposed to Socialism, either in whole or in part, and regard it as an unconstitutional usurpation of power and a denial of the right of private property for government to own or operate the means of producing and distributing goods and services in competition

with private enterprise, or to regiment owners in the legitimate use of private property."

Ezra Taft Benson

Ezra Taft Benson, God, *Family, Country: Our Three Great Loyalties* (SLC: Deseret Book, 1974), 300.

"We have urged you, above all, to try to support good and conscientious candidates of either party who are aware of the great dangers inherent in communism and who are truly dedicated to the constitution in the tradition of our fathers. We have suggested also that you should support candidates who pledge their sincere fidelity to our liberty – a liberty which aims at the preservation of both personal and property rights."

David O. McKay

Donald Q. Cannon, ed., *Latter-day Prophets and the United States Constitution,* (Provo, Utah: Religious Studies Center, Brigham Young University, 1991), 116–33.

FROM THE SCRIPTURES:

"And God blessed them, and God said unto them, Be fruitful, and multiply, and replenish the earth, and subdue it: and have dominion over the fish of the sea, and over the fowl of the air, and over every living thing that moveth upon the earth. And God said, Behold I have given you every herb bearing seed, which is upon the face of all the earth, and every tree, in the which is the fruit of a tree yielding seed; to you it shall be for meat."

Genesis 1:28

"Thou shalt not steal. . . . Thou shalt not covet thy neighbour's house. . . nor his ox nor his ass, nor any thing that is thy neighbour's." (It is impossible to steal or covet something that does not rightfully belong to someone else.)

Exodus 20:15, 17

"And you are to be equal, or in other words, you are to have equal claims on the properties, for the benefit of managing the concerns of your stewardships, every man according to his wants and his needs, inasmuch as his wants are just – And all this for the benefit of the church of the living God, that every man may improve upon his talent, that every man may gain other talents, yea, even an hundred fold, to be cast into the Lord's storehouse, to become the common property of the whole church – Every man seeking the interest of his neighbor, and doing all things with an eye single to the glory of God."

Doctrine and Covenants 82:17-19

Author's Note: *Concerned for others by choice, not by force. Individual ownership of talents and motives to improve talents and willingly give extra fruits to the church.*

PROPER ROLE OF GOVERNMENT

FROM THE CONSTITUTION:

The proper role of government is understood better when one considers the colonists' grievances against Great Britain as listed in the Declaration of Independence and the remedies that were written into the Constitution and the first 10 amendments, otherwise known as the Bill of Rights.

"The powers not delegated to the United States by the Constitution, nor prohibited by it to the States, are reserved to the States respectively, or to the people."

10th Amendment

"The enumeration in the Constitution, of certain rights shall not be construed to deny or disparage others retained by the people."

9th Amendment

"Deriving their just powers from the consent of the governed."

Declaration of Independence

FROM THE FOUNDING FATHERS:

"To relieve the misfortunes of our fellow-creatures is concurring with Deity; it is godlike; but, if we provide encouragement for laziness, and supports for folly, may we not be found fighting against the order of God and nature, which, perhaps, has appointed want and misery as the proper punishments for, and cautions against, as well as necessary consequences of, idleness and extravagance? Whenever we attempt to amend the schemes of Providence and to interfere with the government of the world we had need be very circumspect, lest we do more harm than good."

Benjamin Franklin

Methodist Episcopal Church, *Southern Methodist Review, Vol. 57, Issue 3* (Nashville, TN: 1908), 493.

"The rapid advancement of the executive authority is a topic which has already been alluded to.... I believe the power of the executive has increased, is increasing, and ought now to be brought back within its ancient constitutional limits...

"I have nothing to do with the motives which have led to those acts, which I believe to have transcended the boundaries of the Constitution. Good motives may always be assumed, as bad motives may always be imputed. Good intentions will always be pleaded for every assumption of power; but they cannot justify it, even if we were sure that they existed. It is hardly too strong to say, that the Constitution was made to guard the people against the dangers of good intention, real or pretended. When bad intentions are badly avowed, the people will promptly take care of themselves. On the other hand, they will always be asked why they should resist or question that exercise of power which is so fair in its object, so plausible and patriotic in appearance, and which has the public good alone confessedly in view? Human beings, we may be assured, will generally exercise power when they can get it; and they will exercise it most undoubtedly, in popular governments, under pretences of public safety or high public interest. It may be very possible that good intentions really do exist when constitutional restraints are disregarded. There are men, in all ages, who mean to exercise power usefully; but who mean to exercise it. They mean to govern well, but they mean to govern. They promise to be kind masters; but they mean to be masters. They think there need be but little restraint upon themselves. Their notion of the public interest is apt to be quite closely connected with their own exercise of authority. They may not, indeed, always understand their own motives. The love of power may sink too deep in their own hearts even for their own scrutiny, and may pass with themselves for mere patriotism and benevolence."

Daniel Webster *(not a founding father, but a great quote)*

Edwin P. Whipple, *The Great Speeches and Orations of Daniel Webster* (Boston: Little, Brown, and Co, 1886), 430-431.

"The power under the Constitution will always be in the people. It is entrusted for certain defined purposes, and for a certain limited period, to representatives of their own choosing and whenever it is exercised contrary to their interest, or not agreeable to their wishes, that their servants can and undoubtedly will be recalled."

George Washington

F. M. Robinson, ed., 1787. Letter to Bushrod Washington (Baltimore: United States Naval Institute Proceedings, 1922), 426.

"Government is not reason; it is not eloquence; it is force! Like fire, it is a dangerous servant and a fearful master."

George Washington

Warren L. McFerran, *The Principles of Constitutional Government: Political Sovereignty* (Gretna, LA: Pelican Publishing Co., 2009), 12.

"I am for doing good to the poor, but I differ in opinion about the means. I think the best way of doing good to the poor, is not making them easy *in* poverty, but leading or driving them *out* of it . . . I observed in different countries, that the more public provisions were made for the poor, the less they provided for themselves, and, of course became poorer. And, on the contrary, the less was done for them, the more they did for themselves, and became richer."

Benjamin Franklin

Benjamin Franklin, *Memoirs of Benjamin Franklin, vol. 2* (New York: Harper and Brothers, 1839), 85.

FROM THE PROPHETS:

One of the greatest documents written on this principle bears its name, The Proper Role of Government, by Ezra Taft Benson. It is as good as it gets and I would highly recommend a thorough reading of it. It is available online and in print through various outlets.

"The Constitution of the United States and of this State . . . are not dangerous to good men; they are only so to bad men who are breakers of the law. ...Shall we longer bear these cruelties which have been heaped upon us for the last ten years in the face of heaven, and in open violation of the constitution and law of these United States and of this

State? God forbid! I will not bear it: If they take away my rights, I will fight for them manfully and righteously until I am used up. We have done nothing against the rights of others."

Joseph Smith

F.D. Richards, *Journal of Discourses, vol. 2* (Liverpool, 1855), 167-168.

"The Constitution and the laws that have been enacted under its provisions are calculated to insure liberty, not license, to all who dwell here." (Liberty = freedom to do good; License = permission to act)

George Albert Smith

Donald Q. Cannon, ed., *Latter-day Prophets and the United States Constitution,* (Provo, Utah: Religious Studies Center, Brigham Young University, 1991), 100–15.

FROM THE SCRIPTURES:

"We do not believe that human law has a right to interfere in prescribing rules of worship to bind the consciences of men, nor dictate forms for public or private devotion; that the civil magistrate should restrain crime, but never control conscience; should punish guilt, but never suppress the freedom of the soul. We believe that all men are bound to sustain and uphold the respective governments in which they reside while protected in their inherent and inalienable rights by the laws of such governments; and that sedition and rebellion are unbecoming every citizen thus protected, and should be punished accordingly; and that all governments have a right to enact such laws as in their own judgments are best calculated to secure the public interest; at the same time, however, holding sacred the freedom of conscience. We believe that every man should be honored in his station, rulers and magistrates as such, being placed for the protection of the innocent and the punishment of the guilty; and that to the laws all men show respect and deference, as without them peace and harmony would be supplanted by anarchy and terror; human laws being instituted for the express purpose of regulating our interests as individuals and nations, between man and man; and divine laws given of heaven, prescribing rules on spiritual concerns, for faith and worship, both to be answered by man to his Maker. We believe that the commission of crime should be punished according to the nature of the offense."

Doctrine and Covenants 134:4-6, 8

REPUBLICAN GOVERNMENT

FROM THE CONSTITUTION:

"This Constitution, and the Laws of the United States *which shall be made in Pursuance thereof*... shall be the supreme Law of the Land." (*Laws have to be made to follow the Constitution otherwise they are not the supreme law of the land.*)

Article VI, Clause 2

"[The Congress shall have Power] to make all Laws which shall be necessary and proper for carrying into Execution the foregoing Powers." *(Government isn't the judge of what necessary and proper refers to. The laws must be tied directly to the listed powers preceding clause 18 which are explicit and defined.)*

Article I, Section 8, Clause 18

FROM THE FOUNDING FATHERS:

"The end of law is not to abolish or restrain, but to preserve and enlarge freedom. For in all the states of created beings, capable of laws, where there is no law there is no freedom. For liberty is to be free from restraint and violence from others, which cannot be where there is no law."

John Locke *(not a founding father, but a great quote)*

John Locke, *Two Treatises on Government* (London: Bettesworth, Pemberton and Symon, , 1728), 179.

"That in tracing these evils to their origin every man had found it in the turbulence and follies of democracy."

Edmund Randolph

Max Farrand, ed., *The Records of the Federal Convention of 1787, vol. 1,* (New Haven: Yale University Press, 1911), 51.

"As there is a degree of depravity in mankind which requires a certain degree of circumspection and distrust: So there are other qualities in human nature, which justify a certain portion of esteem and confidence. Republican government presupposes the existence of these qualities in a higher degree than any other form."

James Madison

James Madison, *The Federalist Papers, #55* (New York : Cosimo Classics, 2006), 365.

"We are now forming a republican government. Real liberty is never found in despotism or the extremes of democracy, but in moderate governments. ... if we *incline too much to democracy, we shall soon shoot into a monarchy.*"

Alexander Hamilton

Henry Cabot Lodge, ed., *The Works of Alexander Hamilton* (New York: G.P Putnam's Sons, 1904), 411.

"Law is defined to be a rule of action; but how can that be a rule, which is little known, and less fixed?"

James Madison

James Madison, *The Federalist Papers, #62* (New York : Cosimo Classics, 2006), 406.

"But I go on this great republican principle, that the people will have virtue and intelligence to select men of virtue and wisdom. Is there no virtue among us? If there be not, we are in a wretched situation. No theoretical checks — no form of government can render us secure. To suppose that any form of government will secure liberty or happiness without any virtue in the people, is a chimerical idea. If there be sufficient virtue and intelligence in the community, it will be exercised in the selection of these men [to Congress]. So that we do not depend on their virtue, or put confidence in our rulers, but in the people who are to choose them."

James Madison

William T. Hutchinson, ed., *The Papers of James Madison, Vol. 11* (Chicago and London: University of Chicago Press, 1962), 163.

FROM THE PROPHETS:

"The position of this church on the subject of communism has never changed. We consider it the greatest satanical threat to peace, prosperity and the spread of God's work among men that exists on the face of this earth."

David O. McKay

David O. McKay, *Conference Report* (SLC: The Church of Jesus Christ of Latter-day Saints, April 1966), 109.

"God provided that in this land of liberty, our political allegiance shall run not to individuals, that is, to government officials, no matter how great or how small they may be. Under His plan our allegiance and the only allegiance we owe as citizens or denizens of the United States, runs to our inspired Constitution which God Himself set up. So runs the oath of office of those who participate in government. A certain loyalty we do owe to the office which a man holds, but even here we owe, just by reason of our citizenship, no loyalty to the man himself. In other countries it is to the individual that allegiance runs. This principle of allegiance to the Constitution is basic to our freedom. It is one of the great principles that distinguishes this 'land of liberty' from other countries."

J. Reuben Clark, Jr.

J. Reuben Clark Jr., *Conference Report* (SLC: The Church of Jesus Christ of Latter-day Saints, October 1963), 15-19.

"I stand for Constitutional law, and if any transgress, let them be tried by it, and, if guilty, suffer its penalty."

Brigham Young

Daniel H. Wells, *Brigham Young Journal of Discourses, Vol. 10* (Liverpool: 1865), 109.

"There are some fundamental principles of this Republic which, like eternal truths, never get out of date, and which are applicable at all times to liberty-loving peoples. Such are the underlying principles of the Constitution, a document framed by patriotic, freedom-loving men…"

David O. McKay

Donald Q. Cannon, ed., *Latter-day Prophets and the United States Constitution* (Provo, Utah: Religious Studies Center, Brigham Young University, 1991), 116–33.

"The wisdom of these provisions in the Constitution which protect the liberties and inherent rights of the citizens, should be apparent to all. They should be guarded and protected with a jealous care. The Constitution is our assurance against anarchy and despotism."

Joseph Fielding Smith

Donald Q. Cannon, ed., *Latter-day Prophets and the United States Constitution* (Provo, Utah: Religious Studies Center, Brigham Young University, 1991), 134-43.

"No Latter-day Saint can be true to his country, true to his Church, true to his God, who will violate the laws which relate to the moral welfare and the spiritual advancement of mankind. The Latter-day Saints should uphold the law everywhere. And it is time that all of us – the leaders of this country, the politicians, the statesmen, the leaders in civic affairs in the state and in the cities, as well as parents and private citizens should so speak of and so uphold the constitutional law of the land that there will everywhere be a renewal of respect for it and a revival of the virtues of honor, honesty, and integrity."

David O. McKay

Donald Q. Cannon, ed., *Latter-day Prophets and the United States Constitution* (Provo, Utah: Religious Studies Center, Brigham Young University, 1991), 116–33.

"The three significant words used in the 12th Article of Faith express the proper attitude of the membership of the Church toward law. These words are obey, honor and sustain. . . ."We obey law from a sense of right. We honor law because of its necessity and strength to society. We sustain law by keeping it in good repute."

David O. McKay

Donald Q. Cannon, ed., *Latter-day Prophets and the United States Constitution* (Provo, Utah: Religious Studies Center, Brigham Young University, 1991), 116–33.

"Even now the form of the Government of the United States differs but little from that of the kingdom of God."

Brigham Young

Asa Calkin, *Brigham Young Journal of Discourses, vol. 6* (Liverpool: 1859), 345.

"I do not lift my voice against the great and glorious Government guaranteed to every citizen by our Constitution, but against those corrupt administrators who trample the Constitution and just laws under their feet. They care no more about them than they do about the Government of France; but they walk them under their feet with impunity."

Brigham Young

Asa Calkin, *Brigham Young Journal of Discourses, vol. 5* (Liverpool: 1858), 232.

"It was observed this morning that the government of the United States was the best or most wholesome one on the earth, and the best adapted to our condition. That is very true. And if the constitution of the United States, and the laws of the United States, and of the several States, were honored by the officers, by those who sit in judgment and dispense the laws to the people, yes, had even the letter of the law been honored, to say nothing of the spirit of it, of the spirit of right, it would have hung Governors, Judges, Generals, Magistrates, etc., for they violated the laws of their own States..."

Brigham Young

F. D. Richards, *Brigham Young Journal of Discourses, vol. 2* (Liverpool: 1855), 310.

"But to proceed; the principal evil is in the rulers, or those who profess to be rulers, and in the dispensers of the law, and not the Constitution, it is pure."

Brigham Young

F. D. Richards, *Brigham Young Journal of Discourses, vol. 2* (Liverpool: 1855), 184.

"Then do you profess to ignore the laws of the land? No; not unless they are unconstitutional, then I would do it all the time. Whenever the Congress of the United States, for instance, pass[es] a law interfering with my religion, or with my religious rights, I will read a small portion of that instrument called the Constitution of the United States, now almost obsolete, which says "Congress shall pass no law interfering with religion or the free exercise thereof" [US Const. Amend. I]; and I would say, gentlemen, you may go to Gibraltar with your law, and I will live my religion. When you become violators of the Constitution you have sworn before high heaven to uphold, and perjure yourselves before God, then I will maintain the right, and leave you to take the wrong just as you please."

John Taylor

B. Young, *John Taylor Journal of Discourses, vol. 11* (Liverpool: 1867), 343.

"I feel bound to conform my life to the teachings of the Ten Commandments. I feel equally bound to sustain the Constitution of the United States which came from the same source as the Ten Commandments."

George Albert Smith

George Albert Smith, *Conference Report* (SLC: The Church of Jesus Christ of Latter-day Saints, April 1949), 165-171.

"I am saying to you that to me the Constitution of the United States of America is just as much from my Heavenly Father as the Ten Commandments. When that is my feeling, I am not going to go very far away from the Constitution, and I am going to try to keep it where the Lord started it, and not let anti-Christs come into this country that began because people wanted to serve God."

George Albert Smith

George Albert Smith, *Conference Report* (SLC: The Church of Jesus Christ of Latter-day Saints, April 1948), 177-185.

"The preamble to the Constitution does not begin, 'I, the king'; nor does it begin, "I, the President of the United States." It reads . . . "We the people." It was understood that the people would govern; of course, it would have to be by representation, but the control of government would be in the hands of the people. As we read in the Book of Mormon, when the righteous rule, everything is well. King Mosiah gave up his throne with the idea that the people would have a republic, and he called attention to the dangers of a kingdom and a centralized government and the dangers that would arise should the wicked rule."

Joseph Fielding Smith

Joseph Fielding Smith, *Conference Report* (SLC: The Church of Jesus Christ of Latter-day Saints, April 1950), 153-159.

"The question is now whether or not we can make a Republican form of government work, not merely for America but for the world, as all other nations under Heaven may be persuaded of the blessings of freedom enjoyed by the people of this land and to adopt similar governmental systems, thus fulfilling the ancient prophecy of Isaiah, 'that out of Zion might go forth the law and the word of the Lord from Jerusalem' [Isaiah 2:3]."

Harold B. Lee

Donald Q. Cannon, ed., *Latter-day Prophets and the United States Constitution* (Provo, Utah: Religious Studies Center, Brigham Young University, 1991), 144–55.

"We pray that kings and rulers and the peoples of all nations under heaven may be persuaded of the blessings enjoyed by the people of this land by reason of their freedom under thy guidance and be constrained to adopt similar governmental systems, thus to fulfill the ancient prophecy of Isaiah that '. . . out of Zion shall go forth the law, and the word of the Lord from Jerusalem.'"

George Albert Smith

Dedicatory prayer of the Idaho Falls, Idaho Temple, Jan 1, 1950.

"I hope that the membership of this Church will not be deceived into thinking that other plans, other forms of government, other systems of direction whatsoever, are desirable. I want to say to you without any hesitation that no form of government in the world can be compared favorably with the government God gave to us. This is his plan. Then after giving us our civil government, preparing the way for governing ourselves, if you will, he organized the Church and gave it the name of his Beloved Son ..."

George Albert Smith

George Albert Smith, *Conference Report* (SLC: The Church of Jesus Christ of Latter-day Saints, April 1947), 160-167.

"The Constitution under which we live, and which has not only blessed us but has become a model for other constitutions, is our God-inspired national safeguard ensuring freedom and liberty, justice and equality before the law."

Gordon B. Hinckley

Gordon B. Hinckley, "The Times in Which We Live" *Ensign* (2001), 72.

"God's purpose, in raising up these men and inspiring them with daring sufficient to surmount every opposing power, was to prepare the way for the formation of a true Republican government."

Brigham Young

Amasa Lyman, *Brigham Young Journal of Discourses, vol. VII* (Liverpool: 1860), 13.

"We cannot tolerate the sentiment, at one time expressed, by a man, high in authority in the nation. He said: "The Constitution be damned; the popular sentiment of the people is the Constitution!" That is the sentiment of anarchism that has spread to a certain extent, and is spreading over "the land of liberty and home of the brave." We do not tolerate it. Latter-day Saints cannot tolerate such a spirit as this. It is anarchy. It means destruction. It is the spirit of mobocracy, and the Lord knows we have suffered enough from mobocracy, and we do not want any more of it."

Joseph F. Smith

Joseph F. Smith, *The Improvement Era, Vol. 16, No. 2* (Salt Lake City : Young Men's Mutual Improvement Association, 1912), 101.

"We again warn our people in America of the constantly increasing threat against our inspired Constitution and our free institutions set up under it. The same political tenets and philosophies that have brought war and terror in other parts of the world are at work amongst us in America. The proponents thereof are seeking to undermine our own form of government and to set up instead one of the forms of dictatorships now flourishing in other lands. These revolutionists are using a technique that is as old as the human race, — a fervid but false solicitude for the unfortunate over whom they thus gain mastery, and then enslave them.

"They suit their approaches to the particular group they seek to deceive. Among the Latter-day Saints they speak of their philosophy and their plans under it, as an ushering in of the United Order. Communism and all other similar *isms* bear no relationship whatever to the United Order. They are merely the clumsy counterfeits which Satan always devises of the gospel plan. Communism debases the individual and makes him the enslaved tool of the state to whom he must look for sustenance and religion; the United Order exalts the individual, leaves him his property, "according to his family, according to his circumstances and his wants and needs" (D&C 51:3), and provides a system by which he helps care for his less fortunate brethren; the United Order leaves every man free to choose his own religion as his conscience directs. Communism destroys man's God-given free agency: the United Order glorifies it. Latter-day Saints cannot be true to their faith and lend aid, encouragement, or sympathy to any of these false philosophies. They will prove snares to their feet (Jer. 18:22)."

Heber J. Grant, J. Reuben Clark Jr., David O. McKay

Heber J. Grant, J. Reuben Clark Jr., David O. McKay, Letter from the The First Presidency, April, 1942.

FROM THE SCRIPTURES:

"Therefore, choose you by the voice of this people, judges, that ye may be judged *according to the laws* which have been given you by our fathers, which are correct, and which were given them by the hand of the Lord. Now it is not common that the voice of the people desireth anything contrary to that which is right; but it is common for the lesser part of the people to desire that which is not right; therefore this shall ye observe and make it your law–to do your business by the voice of the people. And if the time comes that the voice of the people doth choose iniquity, then is the time that the judgments of God will come upon you; yea, then is the time he will visit you with great destruction even as he has hitherto visited this land" *(At first glance this appears to be a statement in support of democracy, but upon closer re-*

view, it is clear the people were to democratically choose governmental representatives – judges in this case – to administer the government on their behalf.)

Mosiah 29:25-27

"Have mercy, O Lord, upon all the nations of the earth; have mercy upon the rulers of our land; may those principles, which were so honorably and nobly defended, namely, the Constitution of our land, by our fathers, be established forever."

Doctrine and Covenants 109:54

"Therefore thou art condemned to die, according to the law which has been given us by Mosiah, our last king; and it has been acknowledged by this people; therefore this people must abide by the law."

Alma 1:14

"And whosoever has committed iniquity, him have I punished according to the crime which he has committed, according to the law which has been given to us by our fathers."

Mosiah 29:15

"And it came to pass that by thus exercising the law upon them, every man suffering according to that which he had done, they became more still, and durst not commit any wickedness if it were known; therefore, there was much peace among the people of Nephi..."

Alma 1:33

"And he selected a wise man who was among the elders of the church, and gave him power according to the voice of the people, *that he might have power to enact laws according to the laws which had been given*, and to put them in force according to the wickedness and the crimes of the people." (*Italicized portion is another way of stating the supremacy clause – "... the laws of the United States which shall be made in pursuance thereof, shall be the supreme law of the land" (Artilce VI, Clause 2). i.e. laws only have validity if they comply with the supreme law of the land which has already been given*)

Alma 4:16

Appendix

About the Authors

Jeff Hymas is the founder of the non-profit organization, In the Constitution (www.InTheConstitution.org), which has produced numerous resources to help youth and adults alike learn the true principles of freedom found "In the Constitution". Jeff discovered his passion for the Constitution when he was a Human Resource Manager and began heavily researching the effects of the Affordable Care Act on the financial health of the company he worked for. Coinciding with his personal studies, the beautiful principles of freedom that had always seemed important to him were beginning to occupy his thoughts and desires. Those principles took on an integral part of his life when his wife ShaRee convinced him to shadow his state senator to learn more. The senator encouraged Jeff to share what he had learned in his research regarding the ACA at the House and Senate committee hearings regarding an ACA nullification bill the Senator was sponsoring—coincidentally the very week Jeff was shadowing him (maybe not so coincidental!). This sparked Jeff pursuing his passion in educating Americans—especially youth—about the depth and beauty of the principles found in the Constitution. With the support and sacrifice of ShaRee and their children, Jeff has been able to spend the past four years traveling across states teaching his Constitution presentations to thousands of people.

Jeff is a Magna Cum Laude graduate of the Marriott School of Management at BYU and has his MBA from Idaho State University.

ShaRee is attributed as a contributing author for her part in writing the "Adapting to Families" portion of the book and for her wise advice on how the content of the book should be organized. She also invested dozens of hours listening and providing constructive feedback, which resulted in a much better end product. ShaRee also graduated from BYU in Marriage, Family and Human Develepent. Jeff and ShaRee are the happy parents of eight wonderful children.

Marlene Peterson also significantly contributed to this book by compiling twelve pre-1920's stories to help illustrate each principle. Marlene is the founder and president of Libraries of Hope (www.librariesofhope.com) which is dedicated to restoring the lost arts of educating the hearts of children. She has a special love for stories and storytelling. A graduate of BYU in Child Development and Family Relations, she and her husband, Brent, have raised nine children. They currently reside in Appomattox, Virginia, blissfully surrounded by the stories of history.

29209405R10096

Made in the USA
San Bernardino, CA
16 January 2016